TAKING

OUR PLACES

TAKING

OUR PLACES

The Buddhist Path

to Truly

Growing Up

NORMAN FISCHER

HarperSanFrancisco
A Division of HarperCollins*Publishers*

HarperCollins books may be purchased for educational, business, or sales promotional use. For information please write: Special Markets Department, HarperCollins Publishers, Inc., 10 East 53rd Street, New York, NY 10022.

HarperCollins Web site: http://www.harpercollins.com

HarperCollins®, 📖 ®, and HarperSanFrancisco™ are trademarks of HarperCollins Publishers, Inc.

FIRST EDITION

Designed by Jessica Shatan

Library of Congress Cataloging-in-Publication Data is available upon request.
ISBN 0–06–050551–6

03 04 05 06 07 ❖/RRD 10 9 8 7 6 5 4 3 2 1

"All real living is meeting"

MARTIN BUBER

This book is dedicated to

DANIEL, DANIEL, SHONN-MICHEL AND KIERAN,

TO THEIR PARENTS,

AND TO THE SAN FRANCISCO ZEN CENTER COMMUNITY

WHO PROVIDED US WITH

THE PLACE AND OCCASION TO MEET.

—∞—

Contents

RYOKAN'S
TEARS

DOGEN, A THIRTEENTH-CENTURY JAPANESE ZEN MASTER, ASKS, "What is it that appears?"

This is also my question. What is it that appears? Who is it who is alive, in this body, in this world?

Time is strange. We live within it, depend on it, take it for granted, yet it relentlessly passes, and our lives slip through our fingers moment by moment. Where does time come from, and where does it go? How is it that every moment we are different, we grow, we develop, we are born, we die? What are we supposed to be doing with this life?

After many years of grappling with these questions during the course of my long spiritual practice, I have come to have a feeling for their answers. We don't really know what appears, what time is, where it goes. But we are here to try to understand. And we all have our own way of understanding, and of expressing that understanding through the living of our lives.

Each of us has a place in this world. Taking that place, I have come to feel, is our real job as human beings. We are not generic people, we are individuals, and when we appreciate that fact completely and allow ourselves to embrace it and grow into it fully, we see that taking our unique place in this world is the one thing that gives us a sense of ultimate fulfillment.

Bantu tribesmen, it is said, sneak into the rooms of their children as they sleep and whisper in their ears, "Become what you are."

To take our place is to mature, to grow into what we are. Mostly we take maturity for granted, as if it were something that comes quite naturally and completely as our bodies grow and our minds and hearts fill up with life experience. In fact, however, few of us are truly mature individuals; few of us really occupy our places. We are merely living out a dream of maturity, a set of received notions and images that passes for adulthood. What does it really mean to grow up? How do we do the work that will nurture a truly mature heart from which can flow healing words and deeds? Each of our lives depends on our undertaking the exploration that these questions urge us toward. And the mystery is that the whole world depends on each of us to take this human journey.

Taking our places as mature individuals in this world is not work we can do alone. We need others to help us, and we need to help others. For true maturity can never exist self-contained; it is relational, for we are relational beings, co-created each moment with what we come in contact with. Because we change, because we are open to and affected by the world, maturity must involve our capacity to know and love others.

The words of the epigraph to this book, "All real living is meeting," are those of the German Jewish philosopher Martin Buber. He was making the profound observation that when we truly meet one another—beyond our defenses, beyond our preconceptions, beyond our needs and desires—and open ourselves to each other with the courage to step toward one another, then and only then can we be said to be completely alive.

Real maturity is always meeting what's in front of you in this way. Although true maturity may be rare, we are all capable of it and can recognize it when we see it. When our lives are touched by a mature person, we feel it.

The Japanese Zen monk-poet Ryokan had a teenage nephew who was given to misbehavior. The boy's mother didn't know what to do with him, so she asked her brother for help. "You are a priest and a very good person. Maybe if you talk with him it will have some effect."

Ryokan came to the house for dinner. The mother kept waiting for Ryokan to broach the subject of her son's conduct, but the old monk just sat sadly eating. The meal finished, the dishes cleared, Ryokan made to leave. The boy helped the old man on with his sandals. As he was at work with the sandal straps he felt a warm drop fall onto his head. He looked up and saw Ryokan crying silently. After that night the boy no longer misbehaved.

We are all struggling with our own maturity; none of us can claim the job is finished to satisfaction. But we feel for each other, and that feeling softens and opens us, providing more room for us to grow. Although the process of maturing is endless, and all of us are in the midst of it, we can help each other through our human feeling, which is always wiser than we are.

Some years ago I undertook a project to mentor four adolescent boys in our Zen community. The time I spent with these boys became a deep exploration for me. I had already been teaching Zen for many years and had had many fruitful and close relationships with students. Practicing Zen together had been a good method for us to grow as human beings as we worked to understand and preserve an ancient religious tradition. But as I reflected on my Zen teaching in the light of the mentoring relationship I was undertaking with these four boys, a deeper sense of spiritual practice began to appear to me.

Spiritual practice, I gradually came to feel, is in essence the practice of maturity. The spiritual path leads us to the places we are meant to occupy in this world. Robes, chanting, ceremony, meditation, text study, and all the rest may be valuable in their own right, but their real purpose lies in the service of the path toward maturity. In spiritual practice we use these traditional techniques and practices as vehicles to warmly connect us so that we can help each other to find the true, lasting, and ongoing maturity that each of our lives requires.

Since I have come to feel this way about the spiritual path, I find my view corroborated everywhere in the religious literature I study. Truly growing up and into the fullness of our humanity is the great underlying theme of all religious teaching.

Buddhism, along with many other religious traditions, speaks of the possibility of a lasting and truly satisfying happiness that can endure even when times are tough. Such happiness can't come from possessions or accomplishments, for these are transitory and will not suffice at the end of the day when life's questions and contingencies loom large. In the end, secure happiness comes only with the solid feeling we have when we know that we have become the person we were meant to be in this lifetime—that we have matured and used the life we have been given in the best way we could.

When I think about the world of the future, with so many difficult choices ahead, I know that only mature people will be able to deal with what arises. I am heartened by the many people I know—young and old alike—who are concerned with their own maturity and willing to work toward it with full courage and energy. The development of human maturity does take much work and effort. But I am sure we are all capable of doing the work and enjoying its fruits. Maturity can't be hurried or produced on schedule. Growth takes time. We have to steep ourselves for a while, like a good cup of tea. We need to go through what's necessary for us to endure. We need time and commitment. Probably we also need some luck. But most of all we need encouragement and vision and mentors, grownups in our lives who can help.

Our particular lineage of Zen, founded by Shunryu Suzuki Roshi, puts little emphasis on enlightenment. It's not that we are unconcerned about enlightenment or that we are opposed to it. Enlightenment is certainly important. Personally seeing the truth of the teachings, breaking through the habit of self-centeredness, opening out to something much wider, and having some clarity and flexibility—all of this is crucial. But just as important, or more important, as a sign of readiness to teach Zen is a person's simple human maturity. Maybe someone is not very enlightened, or not enlightened at all. But if he or she is mature, it is good enough, for as Suzuki Roshi taught us, it is the ongoing practice, carried out with balance, faith, perseverance, kindness, and willingness to reach out to others, that is the most important thing. To practice like this takes a quiet and stable maturity.

It is humbling to realize what an immense job it is to truly accept the task of being human. There is so much room for growth and improvement, and the journey is endless. When you consider the lives of exemplary human beings—those who, like Jesus or Buddha, gave themselves totally to their paths— you begin to get a feeling for the depth and breadth that is not only possible but called for in each of us. It's a challenge, maybe even an impossible challenge, but one that all of us have to undertake, for our humanness demands it of us and won't let us settle for less.

Really growing up, becoming truly yourself—this takes openness and receptivity, inspiration, a loving heart, stability and persistence, trust in the world and in yourself. It takes a peaceful mind, but also an active, decisive, and courageous mind. It takes knowing how to live, knowing how to choose, and knowing how to share those choices with others.

What I have to say about all of this comes from my practice and experience through the years, but it is certainly not the last word. There is no last word. Maturity must be contemplated by each of us thoughtfully, and through action, as our lives unfold.

One

MEETING

I THINK MOST OF US ARE TERRIFIED BY THE IDEA OF GROWING up—or would be if we ever considered the idea seriously. Mostly we don't. We usually take maturity for granted, as one of life's givens. You reach a certain age, you get out of school, you get a job, maybe you marry or settle down, maybe not, but time goes by and you're a grown-up. You get a diploma, a credit card, a job, a car, a house or apartment. After you acquire these emblematic prizes, each of which feels like a milestone, you are there. You are an adult. What more is there to it than that? We think growing up, becoming a mature human being, is natural, almost biological, something we all do automatically simply by virtue of the passage of years and the natural course of things. Life happens to us and we go along with it, and there we are, grown up, developed, wise people.

But like so many other commonplace notions that people in the past did not particularly feel a need to examine (like getting married and having children, choosing a profession and staying with it your whole life), what it means to be a grown-up is something that we today, for better or worse, are being forced to take a fresh look at as the confusion and dissatisfaction of our culture and of our personal lives becomes ever more apparent.

And when we do contemplate the question of what it really means to be an adult, fear sets in. We recognize that despite our social position or accomplishments, despite our relationships, our education, and our psychological astuteness, we really don't know what we are doing with our lives. Where is our life going? What is the purpose for which we were born, the fulfillment we deeply seek? We look like grown-ups, we talk like grown-ups, maybe we have grown-up bank accounts and grown-up responsibilities—but do we really have any idea what we are about?

And if, after much struggle, we think we know the answers to such questions, we are forced to ask another, more agonizing question: Are we living those answers? Or do our lives, in the light of those answers, seem like afterthoughts, like still unformed story lines?

Questions like these about the real meaning of growing up were on the minds of four couples in our Zen community. They all had sons about the same age, from eleven to thirteen, and they were concerned about the rocky transition into young adulthood the boys would soon be facing as they entered their teenage years and began to move through high school. So the parents began a series of conversations. They started by discussing their own adolescence, which had been rough for all of them. Thirty years ago society was slower and saner, they reflected. There were neighborhoods and churches that more or less worked, or were only just starting not to work. Today, despite school, despite sports, despite a myriad of activities for young people, society lacks the social supports of the past, and so, these parents observed, it is tougher to be an adolescent now than it was then. In a culture that is rushed and fragmented, the influence of movies, music, television, computer games, the online culture, and shopping, becomes pervasive and unchallenged. Home life, with everyone so busy and stressed, can be a struggle. How can young people keep their balance, they wondered, with no role models, and with public morality so ambiguous?

They concluded after many discussions that their sons needed an adult in their lives who could help them work out what it means to be getting ready to grow up. This adult needed to be someone who represented the possibility of growing up in a graceful and meaningful way, and had to be willing to relate to them over time. They felt confident as parents, and they were good parents. But they saw that at this crucial moment in their sons' lives their parenting would not be enough.

These parents asked to meet with me, to explain all this and make their intentions clear. They wanted me to take on the job of mentoring their sons.

It was a compelling request. I had taught high school English a few years before and loved the work, the engagement with the students, but I had had to give it up when I was elected co-abbot of the Zen Center. Here was a chance to get involved with young people again.

But more than this, I had thought deeply and critically about the Zen practice that I had been doing for so many years, particularly about the Zen enlightenment stories. Once I got beyond the intriguing foreignness of the Chinese literary style, I realized with some astonishment that most of the stories turn on the warm relationship between master and disciple. They are less about solitary visionary experience than the saving possibility of human relationship. Yes, in Zen we sit long hours on the meditation cushion. But Zen practice is communal, not solitary. Enlightenment is the fruit not of isolation but of connection. Zen is the practice of compassionate and warmhearted relationship. The parents were asking me to share this practice with their sons, to test its limits.

I thought it over for a week or so. Was there a way I could engage with these four boys, using the question of what it means to grow up as the foundation for a relationship in which we might discover something together?

Of course I said yes. But three important conditions seemed necessary if we were to succeed. First, it was important that the boys choose for themselves to commit to the group. Although the parents were enthusiastic, it wasn't their enthusiasm that mattered. It was reasonable for them to require their sons to attend two or three exploratory meetings. But no ongoing group could be formed unless the boys themselves genuinely wanted it.

Second, the boys would have to have ownership and creative control of the group—not me, and not the parents. I would give the best guidance I could, but if the effort was really about fostering genuine maturity, then we would have to trust that the boys were capable of maturity and would grow into it as the group went on. I knew that virtually all of the activities that young people participate in are set up by adults for the good of the young and I felt that this group should be different.

Finally, the group would have a rule of confidentiality. The boys needed to know that they could think and say what they were really feeling without any fear that I'd communicate it to their parents or that the boys themselves would tell other friends. (For this book I have changed the boys' names and the details of their stories.)

With these conditions agreed to, we were ready to begin. We got started one spring afternoon in my austere office at the Zen Center. There was a Buddha on the altar, Japanese scrolls on the walls, and no chairs. We sat on meditation cushions on the spotless tatami floor. Very quietly.

The boys were nervous. They seemed not to know what to expect or how to behave. Sam seemed especially bewildered. The youngest in the group, he had a round, soft face and body and still looked very much like a child. Sam was shy even in the easiest of circumstances, but in such unfamiliar and intimidating surroundings, he was nearly paralyzed. James, the next oldest boy, tried to look confident, but he was at a loss in this situation, where the social cues that he had come to be very sensitive to in school were not obvious. Rashid, much taller than the other two and a year older, kept glancing around the room, flipping a shock of dyed red hair back from his eyes and shifting around on his seat as if there were ants on it. I don't think the situation made him nervous, though—he was always that way, a little oblivious, constantly in motion. Tony was the oldest member of the group. At thirteen, he already looked like a teenager, and like a teenager, he sat sullen on his cushion, his face smothered in a black look. The four boys had known each other a long time. Tony and Rashid were close friends. Sam and James lived in the same building, although they didn't hang out together much. Although three of the boys had known me all their lives—James had moved to San Francisco only a few years before—none of them had ever really said more than a few words to me.

Tony began the conversation—not in the most helpful way. "I'm only here because my parents made me, but I don't see the point," he began, somewhat testily. "I am way too busy, and it's too far to come. There's traffic this time of day. Besides, if you want to know what I think, I think it's stupid. My parents are always coming up with stuff like this. Especially my mother. She doesn't seem to know how to leave well enough alone."

I had to admire his nerve. And his honesty. Better that than polite acquiescence.

The effect of Tony's words on the other boys was unclear. I couldn't tell whether they disagreed, or agreed but were too polite to say or even nod their heads in assent. So I asked them. One by one they all echoed Tony: they all had busy schedules and were only here because their parents had made them come. They didn't get what this was supposed to be about.

If there was one thing I had learned as a high school teacher it was to give up all preconceptions about any young person's response in a given situation. You never know what that response is going to be, or whether the response you seem to be hearing is actually the response that is meant. And then a day later it might be something else anyway. So I took in what they said without dismay or disappointment. I could understand how they felt, I told them. I was busy, too. As to the point—what we were supposed to be doing together— that was for us to figure out. The question was: What does it mean to grow up? Is that an interesting question, an important question?

It was hard to tell. The boys were indulging in the most common form of adolescent male communication: noncommunication. Then Sam said, pointing to the statue on the altar, "What kind of a Buddha is that?"

Before I could respond, Rashid burst out laughing, nearly falling off his cushion, as though what Sam had just said were the stupidest thing in the world. James laughed explosively, too, and Tony started in with loud exaggerated guffaws. Sam turned bright red and looked as if he were about to cry.

Then, oddly, the laughter died as suddenly as it had begun,

as if in midlaugh they had all simultaneously thought of something deadly serious. The room was perfectly silent for a minute or two.

"That's the Buddha of listening," I said. "It's also the Buddha of kindness."

More silence. I could hear the boys breathing, their faces relaxing, losing their I-am-almost-a-teenager persona, settling into a childlike vulnerability. I felt very tenderly toward them at that moment. Somehow the sudden laughter that had torn a hole in our conversation, and the silence that followed it, had made the air seem thicker. Time seemed to pass more slowly, and the boys seemed different from the way they were when they'd first come in. They were softer, less guarded.

"If we did do this thing," Sam finally said after a very long pause, "what would we actually do?"

Well, I didn't really know. And that was the point—as of that moment, none of us did. There was no program, no plan. We would have to discover it. We would have to try to be like that Buddha—listening to each other, being kind, trying to figure out together what to do. That would probably take a few meetings. Then once we had an idea of what could be done, we could see whether we actually wanted to commit to doing it.

The boys considered this for a moment. My vagueness seemed to throw them off. They weren't used to an adult without a plan. Because their parents were coming on pretty strong about this group, they said, they would be willing to meet a few more times, to see what developed. But they were making no long-term promises.

"The point of all this," I went on, "is to try to explore, to try to understand, what it means to be a grown-up. You might think that I know, or someone else knows, or that it is obvious, but it is not obvious. It's something I hope we can discover. I am not talking about the received notions of adulthood, the magazine or TV ideas of it, or your parents' ideas of it. What do *we*, what do *you*, actually think about it? Have you ever really thought about it before? How would you define growing up? And how does it come about? Just by time going by? What's the difference between being a grown-up and being a child? Are all the adults you know really grown-ups? If not, how can you tell those who are from those who aren't? Is growing up automatic? If not, how do you go about it?

"Do you want to grow up? How will it change you? What will you get out of it and what will you give up? How do you feel about these questions? Are they serious questions? Are you ready for them? Are they questions worth spending time on? Could you take them seriously, not just fool around with them, but somehow engage them with all your heart?"

As the boys sat on their cushions in the quiet room considering all this, I could feel their ambivalence and confusion. They were becoming excited, interested in what I was saying. It awakened something in them to hear all this and to begin to think about it. These questions seemed to be so important and so timely, yet the boys hadn't ever considered them before. But as much as they were enthusiastic about addressing these questions, they also hung back. They seemed gripped by the kind of dread you feel when something you have anticipated or hoped for without thinking about it much is finally, suddenly, about to come to pass.

Like everyone at this age, these four boys had undoubtedly contemplated, each in his own vague and private way, the thought of growing up, but never as though it were something real that would actually take place. And soon. Beginning to seriously explore their thoughts and feelings about it was both exhilarating and terrifying.

14

Two

MATURITY

ONE OF MY EARLIEST MEMORIES IS OF LISTENING TO AN OLD 45rpm record of Bible stories when I was three or four years old. The record terrified and thrilled me, especially in those climactic moments when God entered the story as a resonant, booming, authoritative male voice. At those moments I'd run to a safe hiding place beneath the dining room table. Despite my terror, I loved the God parts of the record and would play them again and again.

I lived in a small town in northeastern Pennsylvania, on the Susquehanna River, with my parents, my grandparents, and my brother. Our family life was ordinary, quiet, stable, and uneventful, except for my grandfather, who was miserably ill and quite vocal about his pain and frustration. Only this experience of God's voice on the record (magnified by the darkness and wonder of a child's imagination) tipped me off to the fact that there were things in this universe that were more compelling and more mysterious than I knew of.

We lived on Main Street in an apartment over my grandparents' tailor shop, far from where other children lived, so I didn't play much with friends. I was a brooding child, full of questions about life and death and given to vague, dark feelings. My main companion was my grandmother, a tiny woman with a peasant build who had been born in an indefinite place in Europe she referred to only as "the old country." She had come to America as a child, was married by arrangement, learned her husband's trade, and eventually ran the business while raising four girls and caring for my ailing grandfather until he died, when I was seven. Spunky and full of humor (she knew the words to hundreds of dance hall songs, which she sang in a variety of ethnic accents), she was a good friend for me. We had long conversations almost every day. Often she would bring up her own death, which she felt would be coming soon, although her health was perfect. "Soon I will be pushing up daisies, you'll see," she would say, and then chuckle. Although it was forbidden (either by the doctor's orders or by the social customs she'd grown up with), she smoked cigarettes—"on the sly," as she put it—and her smoking as we talked together in her room created a conspiratorial air.

When I was in grade school, the musical version of *Peter Pan* appeared on television. The story presents two clearly opposed worlds: Peter's world is full of adventure, danger, drama, and conflict, and the grown-up world (exemplified by Wendy's parents, benign but shadowy figures to whom Wendy eventually returns at the end of the story) is safe but boring, reassuring but banal. I was impressed with Peter's powerful vow in the striking musical number "I Won't Grow Up." Somehow this anthem struck a chord with me, resonating perfectly with the sense that I was beginning to develop, as I watched the grown-ups around me, that adulthood was a distinctly disappointing proposition. Although you might gain power in achieving it, you lost imagination and nerve—not a very good trade-off it seemed to me. I felt instinctively the huge gap between adult and childhood life, and I was loyal to the latter, especially since, as in the story of Peter Pan, the adults always won out in the end.

A romantic, I loved lost causes. Peter's vow became mine, and I repeated it to myself frequently. *I won't grow up. I won't change. I will never abandon the feelings and thoughts that I have now.* Of course I soon forgot about this vow, but later on, during the turmoil of my adolescence, I remembered the vow, and it seemed more compelling and more serious then than ever before.

Some might well argue that this impossible vow not to grow up is a pathetic cry of fear and avoidance. I suppose this is possible, but that wasn't what it felt like. To me, the vow to never grow up was a commitment to a quest for truth and courage in living. I was determined not to let practical considerations deter me from this quest.

Conscious of my own budding personhood—what I came to feel was the challenge, the problem, of being myself—I began to develop a critical eye toward the world. I looked at my parents, at their friends, at my relatives, and found them all seriously lacking. I began to feel that none of the adults I knew had any interest in what naturally interested me: excitement, growth, development. They seemed to have given up on life's dynamic challenges long ago, and were now just trying to survive, raise their families, earn a living, get by. Their bearing and conduct seemed to express timidity and reluctance, a fearfulness about life. They seemed resigned rather than engaged, and safety seemed to be their crucial and overriding concern.

Although I now participate in and have a great respect for the Jewish tradition in which I was raised, at the time it never occurred to me that religion had any answers for me. Judaism, as I saw it then, was just something Jewish people did as a matter of course. If anything, it seemed only to contribute to the dullness of the adult world.

I went away to college and found the world outside my small town to be exotic, full of ideas I knew nothing about. I was soon devouring books on literature, religion, and philosophy and gravitating toward people whom I could discuss them with. Reading the existentialist philosophers, who were popular then, led me to a book on Zen by the Japanese scholar D. T. Suzuki, who had recently made such a big impact when he taught at Columbia University. Suzuki's book confirmed for me that, yes, just as I was beginning to feel, the world was indeed a wreck, and the people in it fundamentally confused. No one, not even God, was going to fix it. The optimistic American worldview that I had grown up with was definitely naive. Things were not getting better, they were getting worse, and not only did no one know what to do about it, very few even recognized what was happening! And now we had nuclear weapons in our hands, and we were locked in a conflict to the death with the Soviet Union. It seemed we were headed for certain disaster.

On the other hand, we didn't have to succumb to despair. Instead, Suzuki's Zen message seemed to offer a radically new vision of existence, an opening beyond logic and expectation. The world might look rootless and out of control, but the fault was in our own eye, not in the world, his words implied. If only we could see the world as it truly was, if we could open the inner eye, we'd see that beyond our confusion and the world's suffering was a deeper acceptance and perfection, a profound and dynamic peacefulness even in the midst of trouble that made energetic and imaginative engagement with the world possible. This was Zen enlightenment, a sudden and transformative opening to the truth.

I was an instant convert. Enlightenment was surely the answer to this impossible situation. I assumed, as Suzuki's books seemed to imply, that once I was enlightened everything would be clear and simple. I would be cured. I would find a way to live in the world happily and effectively. Little did I suspect that enlightenment would be the challenge of each and every moment of my life and that I was embarking, without knowing what I was doing, on the path of Zen practice, an everyday affair that I would be engaged in meticulously and with heart for a lifetime.

In Mahayana Buddhism, of which Zen is a school, the ideal practitioner is called a *bodhisattva*, literally an "awakening" or "enlightening" being. A bodhisattva is a Buddha in process, someone who is eagerly working on enlightenment, practicing acts of goodness and devotion, studying the teachings, and always aspiring to fully develop all good qualities. The bodhisattva path includes the diligent practice of six virtues: generosity, ethical conduct, enthusiastic energy, patient endurance, meditation, and transcendent wisdom.

But the defining characteristic of bodhisattvas is altruism. Bodhisattvas are awakening beings not only because they themselves are aiming toward awakening, but because their aim is to awaken other beings. This compassionate wish is their primary motivation, and forming, developing, nurturing, and strengthening this wish until it takes on the force of a vow is the essence of a bodhisattva's path.

Bodhisattvas understand the hidden secret of awakening: there can be no self-awakening without the awakening of others. The practice of the Way and the realization of its truth can be accomplished only with the help of others, through helping others. It is only by aiding others with a warm hand

and a warm heart that the bodhisattvas can accomplish their own spiritual work. So the word *bodhisattva* always implies compassion and altruism. Bodhisattvas can't be self-centered. Always concerned for others, they try to help bring others further along on the path.

I have always been struck by the language the sutras use to describe bodhisattvic altruistic activity: the bodhisattva *matures beings,* the sutras say. The work of the bodhisattva is, in other words, to become mature and in doing so to work for the maturity of others.

In doing this work, bodhisattvas must be supremely practical. They must understand the infinite variety of human circumstances and how to harmonize with and master those circumstances for the sake of maturing others. This is called the "skillful means" of the bodhisattvas. If someone needs house repairs, the bodhisattva appears as a carpenter; if someone has a clogged toilet, the bodhisattva appears as a plumber; if someone is sick, the bodhisattva appears as a doctor or as medicine. If a person is hungry, the bodhisattva provides food. If a person is cold, the bodhisattva brings a blanket, a fire, or a space heater.

Studying the implications of these teachings over the years, I came to appreciate that there is a way of becoming truly mature—spiritually, psychologically, and emotionally—without closing down, without resignation, without a loss of delight, and without ever giving up devotion to the pursuit of truth. In fact, I came to feel that the pursuit of truth with rigor, determination, courage, commitment, discipline, joy, and kindness must be what real maturity is all about. How could it be otherwise? And I saw that the maturity of the bodhisattva isn't opposed to a practical everyday life. In fact, such maturity requires a practical everyday life—one lived with energy, kindness, and responsibility—as the training ground for developing the skillful means necessary to complete the endless task of enlightening all beings.

And this is how I eventually came to see that, paradoxically, my vow never to grow up and my vow as a Zen practitioner to become mature myself and to work to mature others were quite compatible. In fact, in true Zen dialectical fashion, these two vows were necessary mirrors for each other. *Not to grow up*, not to drop the endless search for truth because it is too difficult or too risky or too impractical or too costly, really meant *to grow up*, to become a person capable of true responsibility and real love because true responsibility and real love depend on a constant involvement with the truth.

Still in my twenties, I married and had children. At first I found being a husband and a father quite difficult, but soon I saw that the daily challenges of loving someone and backing up that love with loving conduct were worthy of my truth-seeking spirit. Like most of us, I had to work at this. I was shocked, as new fathers usually are, to discover how demanding it is to care for a child, and how much cooperation it requires. Resting comfortably at the end of the day while my wife had everything under control was not in the cards. She was more tired than I was and needed my help as soon as I came home from work. This relentless activity took some getting used to for both of us and produced a certain amount of panic and resentment in me, but it got easier once I decided to see the responsibilities of daily life as a challenge to my bodhisattva practice (I could work on developing enthusiastic energy and patience) rather than as an unmitigated burden. My skillful means was to use the time walking from my car up the steps to our apartment as meditation time, time to refresh myself and get ready to help. I never really mastered this, but it was my daily effort, and as time went on I got better at it.

Thinking about Martin Buber's wonderful statement that "all real living is meeting," we can appreciate that life is nothing but a series of encounters, and that we are always provided, whether we know it or not and whether we like it or not, with a clear choice: Do I move into this moment of meeting, or do I shrink away from it because it may require too much of me? Responsibility is a cornerstone of maturity, but it need not appear as a heavy weight. For a bodhisattva, responsibility appears as a willingness to move into what occurs with full attention, to move into each person, each event, each moment, good or bad, like it or not, and to take on each encounter as a challenge. Recognizing this (with much help from my Zen teachers and my wife and sons), I began to grow up.

It's important to note that the sort of growing up that was beginning to take place in my life at that time, and that I wanted to share later with the four boys in our mentoring group, goes against the grain of our culture. For bodhisattvas, maturity is waking up to what's real even if it doesn't meet our desires and expectations. But America isn't about waking up; on the contrary, it has always been a place for dreaming. We say so pretty clearly when we say that we believe in the American dream. We speak of this dream positively, and politicians run for office on the strength of it.

From our beginnings as a nation, the dream has been central. The earliest settlers, devoted readers of the Bible, saw the New World as the promised land. Their faith was that America was the new Jerusalem, a fresh start, God's country, a place where things that had been impossible elsewhere would become possible. This founding sense of America's supernatural promise became legendary: generations of immigrants saw America as a place of boundless opportunity, a land where there was always room, where wealth, success, and fame could be achieved at any time regardless of who you were or where you came from, where if you failed you could always try again until you succeeded. You could depart from another country where there was suffering and difficulty (as my grandparents had done), arrive here, and escape all the misery of the old country, simply leave it behind forever. The "old country" would become the past, something hardly worth thinking about anymore. (The American dream was not available to those peoples who did not come here seeking it: African Americans, who were forcibly brought here, and Native Americans, who were forcibly displaced. The experience of these peoples has always provided a sobering dose of reality that stands in sharp counterpoint to the dream.)

We live in a child's fairy tale when we deny difficulty and fantasize that trouble will simply dissolve behind us when we leave it and believe that from now on things will always— *should* always—work out just fine. With such a vision, we suffer deeply when things go wrong. Adversity is unthinkable, unacceptable. Should it come, it must be our fault, our personal failing, and we don't want to admit this. It's too painful to fail when everyone else is succeeding so brilliantly (or so we are told). Instead, we pretend that everything is fine, everything is only getting better, this temporary setback is no problem at all, we'll have things right in no time.

Denying difficulty, we never learn that difficulty can be creative and fruitful. This national habit of denial of difficulty does not foster a climate in which maturity can grow. It encourages us all to be children for our whole lives, to be self-deceitful and surface-oriented, skimming along on the slick bubble of the dream, which is terribly fragile exactly because it leaves out the realistic acceptance of life's often drastic actualities. It is no wonder that there is so much suffering in our culture, despite our wealth and power. So many of us seem not to know how to face life as it really is. And therefore we find it very difficult to grow up.

That's the downside of the American dream, and it is a very serious one. But the American dream is also wonderful. The dream keeps us innocent, flexible, and energetic, qualities that have produced our immense national success. Because of the dream, we believe that freedom, democracy, and fair-mindedness are always possible, and we are willing to sacrifice to protect them. Because of the dream, we are inspired by wild and immense spaces untouched by human hands, and we want to preserve such spaces—our forests, mountains, and skies. This hopeful, energetic, almost naive American spirit provides a wonderful basis for a marvelous and open sort of maturity, which is the potential we have. But we haven't realized it yet.

I suppose that most of us think of maturity as simply a matter of timing. Seeds grow into seedlings, seedlings into plants, and plants bear fruit. All living things develop naturally, and people do, too, coming to a stage of possibility, competence, or ripeness when they are ready to. Of course we grow up. Time passes, the body changes, the mind changes, the emotions change. We become adults.

But this natural maturity, though basic and important, doesn't really make us grown-ups. It is only a beginning, a necessary foundation. Beyond this there must also be emotional maturity, spiritual maturity, and maturity of character. This deeper sort of maturity doesn't come naturally. Many of us never develop it, for it takes a particular kind of thoughtfulness and care beyond what is natural and socially established as a minimal standard for adulthood.

This deeper and more subtle growth requires a fuller vision of maturity, a firm and clear commitment to move toward that vision, and a context and a vehicle for getting there. Here was where the boys and I had work to do, if we could figure out how to do it. We had to find a way to discover and evoke this deeper sense of maturity so that it could become real to us. It couldn't be something that I was presumed to have in me and could therefore pass on to them, like liquid that can be poured from one bottle into another. I could make speeches at them if I wanted to, but what good would that do? They had heard enough speeches in their lives already. And what good would it do me to repeat to them things I thought I knew about life? No, mutual discovery was the only pathway, for them and for me. We would have to enter exploratory ground together, traveling fresh, without assuming anything. The vital question, for me as much as for them, became: What is true maturity, anyway?

It's a good question, one that needs to be pondered for a long time. There are answers to life's most important questions, but they are never final; they change as we change. Maybe true maturity is finding a way of keeping such questions alive throughout our lifetime. For when there are no more questions, we stop maturing and begin merely to age.

To explore this question of maturity, the boys and I thought of people we knew who we felt were truly grown up, and tried to discover what it was about those people that made them seem grown up to us. Out of these discussions we began to develop a working list of qualities that we felt were present in most people whose emotional and spiritual lives were deeply mature. Most of these people, we found, seemed to be responsible without being boring, experienced without being closed-minded, self-accepting without being shut off to change and improvement, loving without being corny, stable without being inert, and strong without being brittle. We discussed all of these qualities at length, being as concrete and personal as possible. Out of our conversations came, eventually, a rough list of qualities that we felt marked a mature person—qualities we felt we wanted to study and point toward in our efforts to truly become grown-ups. The first of these qualities was responsibility.

When the topic of responsibility comes up, I find myself suddenly seized with an attack of scruples and am inspired to speak in a deep, archetypal, stentorian voice (like the voice of God on those childhood records) that trails off into vague distances. I suppose this is how most of us view the notion of responsibility—as the opposite of creativity, spontaneity, and growth. No wonder we resist growing up, and no wonder we become boring when it finally seems we must admit that we are adults and had better start acting like it.

But responsibility doesn't have to be like that. In its truest and most literal sense, responsibility is simply the capacity to respond. Being responsible is an inherently lively quality. It is the capacity to react completely and freely to conditions. Being responsible has nothing to do with control and conformity. Quite the contrary, responsibility is the willingness to confront nakedly and clearly what's in front of you on its own terms and to be called forth fresh by what occurs. The Greek root of the word *response* means to offer, to pledge. To be responsible is to offer yourself to what happens to you, to pledge yourself to your life.

Being responsible in this sense isn't easy. Because it is so active and creative, responsibility is the enemy of all forms of laziness. It requires discovery and self-transcendence. To respond with authenticity, to really be present with what your life is, you have to let go of self-concern and preconception as much as possible and be true to your situation. You must have the courage to let yourself be overcome by what happens to you.

This reminds me of the story of one of our Zen Center priests, who arrived at the center in an odd way. Riding his motorcycle in the mountains one day and coming across a dirt road, he decided to see where it led. The road ended up at our monastery, Tassajara, which was just then opening. The young man came in to look around and was so intrigued by what he saw that he decided to stay for a few days, which became a few months, and then a few years. Eventually he ordained, studied traditional carpentry in Japan, and came back to America to help build the Zen Center's finest temple buildings. He had driven down a mountain road only to see what was there, but because he was willing to respond fully to what he encountered and give himself to it completely, his life turned into a life of benefit.

A mature person is someone who is willing to hear the call, no matter how faint or unexpected it may be, and respond. It is not necessary, however, to look around for things to be responsible for if nothing appears. But when something does appear, you are ready to respond with all of your attention and loving care, and with no excuses, no avoidance, no fanfare. You just roll up your sleeves and do it.

In his well-known text *Instructions to the Head Cook,* the Japanese Zen master Dogen recounts the story of a seminal encounter he had with an old Chinese monk who was serving his monastery as head cook. Although Dogen wanted the old monk to stay with him and engage in conversation about religious matters, the old man said he could not. Since he was head cook, it was his duty to go out in the hot sun to dry mushrooms, a job that had to be done immediately so that the mushrooms would be ready for the evening meal. When Dogen implored him to stay and to get an underling to take care of the mushrooms instead, the old man said, "You do not understand. I am head cook. If I do not do this job, who will do it? And if I do not do it now, when will I do it?"

There is a deep simplicity in taking responsibility in this way. The head cook wasn't trying to prove anything, to get credit for anything, or even to accomplish anything. He was simply occupying his place, fulfilling his role. Although we might not be alert enough to notice it, being responsible in this way has reverberations beyond what we can predict or control. For life's endless possibilities arise in response to our passion to give ourselves fully to what we are doing wherever we are. Our tomorrows can neither be saved up nor created out of our heads; they flow out of our present engagement. Responsibility, far from limiting or shutting down our lives, provides the potential for opening. Even if responsibility seems to keep us in one place for a very long time (as with the young priest who rode his motorcycle) or to press our nose to the grindstone (as with the head cook), we don't feel this as restriction. When we give ourselves to our situation we're letting go of preferences and habits and trusting what's in front of us, with faith that it will provide the wisdom we need. To truly be responsible is to recognize that reality is smarter than we are.

Another clear characteristic of maturity—one that any of us would mention—is experience. A grown-up is someone who is experienced and, through having lived long enough to have seen many things, has a point of view and a measure of savvy about how life works. There is certainly no substitute for the experience that accumulates as the years go by, but it is also possible to be alive for a long time and not really experience our living, not really see our life. The human capacity for self-deception and blindness runs deep. We may be alive, but we have not necessarily lived. If we accumulate experiences without really engaging with them, then our experience tends to make us stodgy and boring. As we catalog and define our experiences, possessing them without ever really being possessed by them, we begin to expect that new situations will just be repetitions of old ones. Soon we feel as if we've seen it all before. We know what to expect. Our point of view gradually becomes a set of blinders rather than a searching flashlight.

But if we pay close and open attention to our experiences, life's larger patterns begin to come into view. We see that all things are transitory and unique. Nothing repeats. We understand that, though always instructive, the past can never tell us what the future will be. Within the larger pattern that experience reveals, there are endless variations. Insofar as we see this, our experience increases our wonder at and appreciation of all that happens. With little life experience, we might be naively excited by the novelty of a person we meet or an event that occurs. But when we truly appreciate our experience, we respond to that newness with a deeper understanding of its meaning and wonder as we relate it to what we have seen before. Far from dampening our sense of wonder, real experience refreshes and mellows it.

Some years ago I attended a peace conference in Belfast, Northern Ireland, with His Holiness the Dalai Lama. We were sitting in a large auditorium listening to the stories of people who had been victims of what is called in Ireland "the troubles," the long, violent conflict between Protestants and Catholics. One person was blind. One was wheelchair-bound. Another was emotionally scarred from having seen his father shot down before his own eyes when he was a child. When I glanced over at His Holiness, I saw that he was weeping like a baby, leaning his head on his assistant's shoulder. A few moments later he was being photographed with two Irish religious leaders, one a Catholic priest, the other a Protestant minister. It happened that both men had bushy white beards. For some reason His Holiness thought this was very funny, so he reached up and gave their beards a tug. I remember that he almost fell off the podium with laughter. The next day the *Irish Times* carried a front-page color picture of the Dalai Lama laughing hysterically while "bearding" the two shocked clergymen. It seemed amazing to me that His Holiness could be so shattered with sadness one moment, and then so freely—almost inappropriately!—merry the next. A man who has seen and felt so much, and who carries a great burden of responsibility, the Dalai Lama nevertheless seems to hold his experience lightly.

We often think of growing up as a slow and inevitable process of dying to life, something to be avoided for as long as possible. We contrast maturity with childhood or youth, which we see as full of excitement and promise. Certainly we encounter a lot of sadness as life goes on. The older we get, the more trouble we've seen, and there's no doubt that life will show us the face of loss. Time passes, youth fades, and people disappear from our lives. And time will also introduce us to bitterness, disappointment, and defeat.

But it is exactly in digesting and accepting the profundity of our difficulties that life opens up to us. The truly experienced person knows and feels the preciousness, fragility, and impermanence of life. Certainly the Dalai Lama has known his share of suffering and has taken it in with all seriousness. But the experience of suffering hasn't dampened his enjoyment of life.

In Japanese culture the appreciation of life—of the beauty of a flower, the peacefulness of a shrine, the purity of a mountaintop scene—seems to be tied to a recognition of impermanence. Often life's most moving moments are found right in the middle of sadness and loss. The twelfth-century Japanese Buddhist poet Saigyo penned this verse:

Winter has withered
Everything in this mountain place:
Dignity is in
Its desolation now, and beauty
In the cold clarity of its moon

Self-acceptance is another key quality of the mature person. Someone who lives long enough, and with enough heart, to truly understand his or her experience, will gradually come to self-acceptance. Observing accurately and without shame our thoughts, deeds, and feelings over time, we begin to see a clearer picture of our character. We let go of our expectations and illusions about ourselves and settle with confidence, into who we really are. As we become familiar with our weaknesses and all the trouble they have caused us, we are less dismayed at them and do not run away from them as often; this new response, in turn, brings us a calmness that helps us stop indulging our weaknesses.

We also come to appreciate our strengths enough to see that we don't have to make a big deal out of them. We don't need to keep reminding ourselves and everyone else about our strengths. Instead we can simply enjoy and make use of them. As time goes on and our self-acceptance deepens, the very idea of strengths and weaknesses seems off the mark because the closer we look, the harder it is to distinguish between the two. All human qualities have a flip side: we're loving, but we meddle; we're fearful, but we're helpfully prudent; we're critical, but we are very perceptive. It's all a dance. As we realize this, it seems increasingly silly to judge ourselves one way or the other.

Still, no matter how well we know ourselves and how much we achieve a steadiness of character, we are never immune to mistakes. With self-acceptance we know this, and we try to make use of our mistakes, learning from them as best we can. Over time we see how often our worst mistakes and most ignominious failures have turned out to be our greatest teachers. Some of our greatest disasters turn out to have powerfully positive consequences for our lives, even though it may take a long time for us to recognize it. Given all of this, we become less worried about making mistakes, although we are regretful when we make them, especially when others are hurt in the process. Zen Master Dogen famously referred to his long life of spiritual endeavor as "one continuous mistake."

Sometimes our mistakes can be helpful to others: if we show that there can be dignity in making mistakes, others can learn from us that they don't have to live in constant fear of error. Many times in my life I have witnessed mistakes that my teachers made—being headstrong or stubborn, being angry when it was inappropriate, being nervous when I wanted them to be clearheaded and cool. Sometimes they said or did things impulsively, or even deliberately, that they shouldn't have said or done. Most of the time I appreciated these mistakes, for they made me see my teacher's humanness and vulnerability. Far from seeing the mistake-making as a flaw that lowered the estimation of my teacher in my eyes, I saw it as a wonderful badge of his or her humanity, which helped me to accept my own imperfection more easily.

I remember the one-hundredth birthday party of my friend and teacher Charlotte Selver, who has been teaching and practicing sensory awareness, a powerful mindfulness training, for more than seventy-five years. After birthday cake and a champagne toast, people gathered around to recount stories from Charlotte's life, incidents that revealed her wisdom. After many tales were told of the wonderful and perceptive things that Charlotte had said or done in the presence of her students, one man said that what he cherished the most were the stupid arguments that Charlotte and Charles, her husband of many years, used to have, often right in the middle of a workshop session. "It was the way you did it," the man said. "So wholeheartedly, without embarrassment or justification. Somehow it gave me permission to be myself without feeling there was some ideal I was supposed to be living up to."

Self-acceptance is paradoxical: we see and accept our essential character, the personality that seems to define us, but at the same time we know that that character is actually in constant flux. When we feel this dynamic interplay between change and constancy and accept the paradox of human character, we see how we can avoid being trapped by ourselves, as so many people are. Since we accept who we are, and are no longer driven to improve, we're not constantly self-critical and off-balance. On the other hand, since we know that who we are isn't fixed but rather is always subtly being reinvented by conditions, we know that we can and will grow and improve if only we pay attention and stay present for what happens to us. With self-acceptance we are confident that we can trust what happens. We begin to realize how much power and subtlety there is in simply seeing ourselves without distortion, without shame, without guilt or desire.

A short and instructive Zen dialogue I am very fond of evokes this profound sense of self-acceptance. A monk named Hui Chao asks his teacher, "What is Buddha?" The teacher replies, "You are Hui Chao." A mature person appreciates the simple fact of being himself or herself, knowing that in the entire cosmos there is now and will only ever be one temporary occurrence of this person. He or she also knows that something deeply unique and necessary is being expressed through his or her life.

Such profound self-acceptance tenderizes the heart, and opens our empathy for others, for we recognize that the precious and unique person we are has been formed and is being formed through our relations with others. We are always creating each other—our moods, our personalities, and our attitudes are always connected to the moods, personalities, and attitudes of others. Experiencing our own suffering without excuse or attempt to escape, we know that others have suffered as we have. Deeply reflecting on all this, we become open to and capable of love. We come to understand the profound truth that there is nothing but love and therefore nothing is more worthwhile, more pervasive, or more necessary.

We think of love as a big enthusiastic feeling. Certainly emotion is part of what love is, but it's not limited to that. Our society's focus on romantic relationships seems natural and delightful, at least if you are in a relationship yourself that is reasonably happy. But love is a much larger container than romance. A person can be loving whether or not he or she is in love with someone. I have many friends who are monks and nuns, among whom are the most loving and mature individuals I know. They are living proof that the power of love, and of loving connection that is deep and satisfying, is a mark of maturity for all of us, regardless of the nature of our relationships.

Love is practical and down-to-earth. It exists in the rough and tumble of real human relationship, with all its problems and misunderstandings. Love requires human warmth and contact. It also requires all the other qualities of maturity I have already discussed—responsibility, experience, and self-acceptance—insofar as we have developed them. Love evokes the healing power of simple human kindness. Mature people are not aloof, coolly distant, or stuck within themselves. They might not all be jolly extroverts, but they all have the capacity to meet others with some degree of warmth and interest.

In my own work with Zen students over the years, I have felt the awesome power of love. Although it may seem extravagant to say so, the truth is that I love the people with whom I practice Zen. I get to know many of them over time and to see their lives unfold, with all the inevitable triumph and tragedy. Sharing all this with them, admiring their courage and sincerity in facing what they face and their determination to keep on devotedly with the practice, how can I not love them? If there is any benefit in our practicing together, all of it comes from this loving relationship, which has a healing power no one can measure or truly understand.

In Zen literature the word *intimacy* is often used as a synonym for enlightenment. In the classical Zen enlightenment stories, a monk or a nun is reduced simultaneously to tears and laughter as he or she suddenly recognizes that nothing in this world is separate, that each and every thing, including one's own self, is nothing but the whole, and that the whole is nothing but the self. What are such stories telling us if not that love is much wider and deeper than an emotion? Love is the fruition of, the true shape of, one's self and all that is.

THE BOYS AND I DISCUSSED THESE AND OTHER QUALITIES that we felt are demonstrated by mature people, but certainly mature people are all different. Some are calm and quiet, others are talky and jumpy. Some are decisive and stubborn, others more thoughtful and softer. Still, it seems that maturity brings stability into a person's life, no matter what that life looks like. When you have lived long enough to find a way of being that suits you, you do become calmer and more stable. When you've learned how to be confident enough to give yourself willingly and completely to what's in front of you, life holds you in place, for you are not off-balance, grabbing for something other than what arises in front of you. You are willing to stand where you are, looking straight ahead without glancing off in a million directions. Some might call this strength of character, but to me it seems more like inspiration. We are inspired by what happens, and what happens deepens us. Life becomes more interesting. Rather than feeling that we have to seek new or exotic experience, we become fascinated with whatever our situation happens to be. We love wherever we are, we love whatever our life provides. Living, just as it is, is enough for us. There's tremendous steadiness and reliability in this acceptance, whatever our personal style of expressing it may be.

I think of my own teacher, Roshi Sojun Weitsman, longtime abbot of the Zen Center in Berkeley, where I began my practice long ago. Sojun is a straightforward and down-to-earth person who, as long as I have known him, has maintained stability in all circumstances. His virtue as a teacher comes from his steadiness. He has been true to the practice for many years and has remained in his seat, so to speak, patiently practicing, no matter what happens, through many changes. He came to Berkeley as a new priest almost forty years ago and simply began to sit meditation, welcoming anyone who wanted to join him. He was there every day, day in and day out, no matter what.

When I was young and having a difficult time in my life, his stability was crucial for me. I was able to sit meditation next to Sojun in the early mornings, and though he said little to me, just seeing him sitting there quietly, and then later in the day steadily going about his business, helped my life. Years went by, and he kept on meditating, kept on being there, kept on taking care of things in a simple way. More and more students came, and now the Zen Center is a thriving community with many seasoned practitioners and teachers. Sojun never calculated about anything or made special efforts to build up the group. He just stayed stably with his practice and continued to give his whole heart to it quietly over the years. And that was enough.

The quality of mature people that is most difficult to understand is strength, because we usually think of strength as toughness or roughness, power or assertiveness. We think of some tough superhero. But mature strength is not like this; it is strength of resolve, the sometimes quiet and sometimes not so quiet courage it takes to stick with what you feel is right and with the course you have decided to take.

Many years ago the meditation hall at Tassajara, our mountain monastery, burned down. It was a rather spectacular event, since the entire community was in the hall doing a ceremony when the fire broke out. We evacuated the building as quickly as possible, without even taking the time to save the precious Buddha statue on the altar. Once outside, we turned back in astonishment to see the old redwood structure completely engulfed in flames. The whole thing happened in the space of a few minutes.

Our community was still young at the time, and losing the meditation hall was the greatest disaster we had ever experienced. The terrible event occurred just as we were making preparations for our most ambitious project, the establishment in San Francisco of Greens, our well-known vegetarian restaurant. This was an enormous undertaking, one that we probably had no right to think we could manage, but our abbot at that time, Richard Baker, felt sure we could do it, and had to do it, not only for the financial support it would provide us but also as an offering to the world. When the meditation hall at Tassajara burned down, we all naturally assumed that the Greens project was off. How could we possibly raise enough money and come up with enough personnel to take on that project as well as the rebuilding of the meditation hall? Clearly it was out of the question. Yet within hours after the fire was put out, Roshi Baker was putting the finishing touches to the architectural plans for Greens, talking to funders and contractors on the telephone, and assuring us that the project would definitely go ahead as scheduled.

When we heard this, many of us thought that the Roshi had gone a bit crazy. Maybe the fire had rattled him so much that he'd lost his judgment. While it might have looked crazy at the time, Roshi Baker's decision turned out to be the right one. Always true to his vision and willing to pay the price to see it through, Roshi Baker had a strength of purpose that was probably the single most important ingredient in the establishing of Greens' success.

Strength of resolve is, however, a tricky thing. It too easily shades off into stubbornness and a pernicious quality of being unyielding. Later on Roshi Baker had many problems at the Zen Center. Things did not turn out well, and it may be that his resolve and strength of purpose contributed to his problems. Real strength is not unyielding. Like a tree that can bend but never break, the strength of a mature person includes flexibility. A mature person has learned through experience that life requires us to be flexible. There is no use insisting that you are right about something. Even if you are, the next minute things may change and you may be wrong. I think of Master Zhaozho, a simple monk who kept his position of leadership not by rigid self-assertion or stubbornness but by quiet and flexibility of word and deed. His strength sometimes appeared as weakness, and there are stories about him that turn on this point. Once a monk came to see him, thinking he was visiting an impressive Zen master. When he saw the unimpressive old master standing before him, the monk rose up to his full height and said, "I came expecting a stone bridge and I only see this rickety wooden one." The master simply replied, "Yes, you see the wooden bridge; you don't see the stone one." No need to shout or contradict. Real strength is like that. It is an inner conviction that transcends external positions or appearances. When you have confidence in your own decisiveness, you can change your mind and not worry about it. When you know your own power, you can be soft without worrying about it. When you know how to stand firm, you can yield when that's the right thing to do.

In Zen there's a dichotomy between two teaching styles called "the grasping way" and "the granting way." The grasping way is tough: it always brings up emptiness and impermanence, never gives the student anything to go on, and withholds for the purpose of fostering the student's independence. The granting way, on the other hand, emphasizes the other side: connection, unity, and warmth. The granting way affirms and encourages the student, helping him or her with constant kindness. These opposing styles are actually not as different as they seem. One depends on the other, and neither can stand without the other. Teachers have always used them both, depending on the student and the situation. To be capable of understanding and manifesting only one side is to misunderstand its nature. To define the granting way as the opposite of the grasping way, or vice versa, and not to see the relationship and interdependence between them, is to make of each teaching style a limitation and a trap. Strength that doesn't know softness and flexibility becomes too brittle and eventually breaks.

In fact, all the qualities of maturity discussed in this chapter can become traps—brittle and limited when we define them too strictly, without subtlety and acuity. When we start to see ourselves as mature in a certain way—as responsible, stable, strong, or experienced, for example—and to judge and order our experience according to one of these prearranged and static concepts, we are already starting to harden and stiffen our experience. As soon as we have a fixed concept of responsibility, true responsibility disappears and we are just trying to be good. As soon as we establish for ourselves a fixed concept of experience and think about how experienced and wise we are, we become dull and incapable of receptivity. Self-acceptance reduced to a fixed concept becomes excessive self-consciousness and self-congratulation. When we reduce love to an idea of love, it dissolves into sentiment. And when we begin to receive awards for our wonderful stability—for doing this for twenty years and that for fifteen years—our stability becomes stodginess and we lose the capacity to change when it is time to.

In a very real and practical sense, then, the important thing is to realize that notions of responsibility, experience, self-acceptance, love, stability, and strength are merely reminders and guideposts to help us keep track of our lives, to encourage us to pay attention and be active by continuing the inner work that we need to do to keep our life lively. Maturity is a matter of making the effort, over time, to be open and sensitive to life. In Zen we call this effort "practice." The most important word in this book, practice is what we do when we foster in our lives a sense of ongoing effort and exploration that isn't just conceptual, but that also involves concrete processes we can work with—and are committed to continue working with—our whole life through. In the rest of this book, I want to discuss some of the practices that can help us achieve maturity.

Three

LISTENING

I STEPPED INTO MY OFFICE FIVE MINUTES LATE FOR OUR meeting. Three of the boys were already there. They were in the midst of an argument.

"You owe me one dollar," James was saying to Tony, with some heat.

"No way," Tony said dismissively.

"You do," Sam said.

Tony slowly turned to face Sam and gave him a withering look. Sam shrank back.

James, his chin trembling, was about to say something else when Rashid burst into the room, disheveled. He looked at the other three boys with a sense of utter disconnection, as if he had never seen them before. They looked at him like an invading force.

Watching all this, I felt invisible, as I often did in the boys' presence. They had a way of being together that was so all-encompassing that anything not within its sphere seemed nonexistent. I resisted the temptation either to ignore them by drifting off or, in schoolteacher fashion, to dispel what was going on and call the meeting to order.

Instead, I listened. I paid close attention to what was going on. I watched the boys' faces, heard their words, observed their body language. As often occurs, my bearing witness in this way served to settle things down. The argument over the dollar, which seemed somehow to be more than an argument over a dollar, dissolved.

Listening with full presence, and with as few preconceptions, notions, or desires as possible, to what was said and to what was not said was crucial to our meetings. And I was not the only one listening—eventually the boys were listening this way as well. Because we were able to do this, the boys began to speak and open up to each other and to me.

Listening is magic: it turns a person from an object outside, opaque or dimly threatening, into an intimate experience, and therefore into a friend. In this way, listening softens and transforms the listener.

Listening is basic and crucial because it is the soil out of which all the fruits of our human relationships grow. Listening takes radical openness to another, and radical openness requires surrender. This is why listening is frightening, although we don't usually think of it that way. It requires a kind of fearless self-confidence that most of us have never developed.

Self-confidence isn't egotism. Egotism is being stuck on yourself, insisting, perhaps quite unconsciously, on seeing everything through the lens of your own interests, your own intelligence, and your own views, capacities, and opinions. With too much egotism, listening is impossible. True self-confidence is different; it isn't confidence in your own superficial self, in your cover story, your views, capabilities, and résumé. It is, on the contrary, the willingness to suspend all of that for a while, in favor of a faith in yourself that goes beyond the surface of who you are. When you are truly self-confident, you are flexible with regard to ego: you can pick up ego when necessary, but you can also put it down when necessary in order to learn something completely new through listening. And if you find that you can't put ego down, at least you know that this is so. You can admit it to yourself. It takes profound self-confidence to be humble enough to recognize your own limitations without self-blame. If you can do that, very soon you will be able to listen.

The next time you are in a conversation pay attention to your listening. Don't just go on automatic pilot. Instead, reflect on what is actually going on. Chances are you will notice that more often than not, when another person is talking, you are not listening. You may be more or less hearing what the person is saying, getting the general drift, but you are probably also preparing or anticipating the remark you will soon be making in rejection of or agreement with what you are hearing. Maybe you interrupt, maybe you lose attention or think about something else, or maybe your mind simply wanders gently off to no place in particular. Daydreaming is a habit so unconscious that it is much more prevalent than any of us realize. Since you are so often not actually listening but rather are absorbed in your own mental habits, you are probably missing out on something, some piece of information, some discovery about yourself or the other person or the world, some *news*.

What's usually in our minds isn't really news. It's the residue of what we've learned, or hoped for, or feared, or been hurt by. Whether we are conscious of it or not, we are almost always strategizing when we engage in conversation with others—trying to find the advantage or to protect ourselves from something foreign or unknown. We aren't listening at all. If we want to survive with some happiness, however, in this world of difference—a world in which we are constantly confronted with one utterly different and unknown person after another (even those we know and live with for many years are sometimes utterly unknown to us)—we had better study the art of listening.

To truly listen is to shed, as much as possible, all of your protective mechanisms, at least for the time of listening. To listen is to be willing to simply be present with what you hear without trying to figure it out or control it. To listen is to be radically receptive to what occurs. To do that, you have to be honest with yourself. You have to be aware of and accepting of your preconceptions, desires, and delusions—all that prevents you from listening. But you also have to be willing to put these preconceptions, desires, and delusions aside so that you can hear what the speaker is saying for what it is. Because truly listening requires that you do this, listening is dangerous. It might cause you to hear something you don't like, to consider its validity, and therefore to think something you never thought before—or to feel something you never felt before, and perhaps never wanted to feel. This feeling might make something happen within you that never happened before. This is the risk of listening, and this is why it is automatic for us not to want to listen.

But listening, however dangerous, is a necessity. If you want to stay open to life and to change, you have to listen. To listen, really listen, is to accord *respect.* Without respect, no human relationship can function normally, for the pain and hurt that inevitably arise from disrespect eventually pervert it. When your mind is occupied (usually quite unconsciously) with your own thoughts and plans and strategies and defenses, you are not listening. And when you are not listening, you are not according respect. The speaker knows this and reacts accordingly.

It doesn't take a psychic to know that someone is not really listening. We all know whether or not we are being listened to. But we are so accustomed to not being listened to that we take it for granted and even see it as normal. This is why it is so startling, and so powerful, almost magical, when we are actually heard by another person within the openness of true listening.

Perhaps the most common and pernicious form of nonlistening is our nonlistening to ourselves. So much of what we actually feel and think is unacceptable to us. We have been conditioned over a lifetime to simply not hear all of our own self-pity, anger, desire, jealousy, wonder. Most of what we take to be our adult response is no more than our unconscious decision not to listen to what goes on inside us. And as with any human relationship, not listening to ourselves damages our self-respect. It occludes the free flow of love from ourselves to ourselves. To allow ourselves to feel what we actually do feel—not to be afraid or dismayed but to open up a space inside our hearts large enough to safely contain what we feel, with the faith that whatever comes up is workable and even necessary—this is what any healthy, mature human being needs to do and what we so often fail to do.

The practice of listening has many depths and many dimensions. In *Zen Mind, Beginner's Mind*, Suzuki Roshi speaks of true listening as emerging from what he calls "beginner's mind"— the mind that is willing to remain receptive and open to surprise. Such a mind is always ready and alert, willing to receive what comes. It has few preconceptions. Unlike the expert's mind, which filters everything through its expertise, beginner's mind is innocent and fertile.

Listening requires beginner's mind, for no one can be an expert on what has never before been heard, in exactly this way, at this precise moment. Listening is being ready to live this moment and willing to confront what's truly new, unhindered by what has happened before. "If your mind is empty, it is always ready for anything; it is open to everything," Suzuki Roshi writes. "In the beginner's mind there are many possibilities; in the expert's mind there are few."

Another expression in Zen for this fertile, empty, listening mind is "I don't know mind." The statement "I don't know" doesn't signify ignorance or stupidity or even humility; rather, it points to this kind of ready, fertile, receptive mind that has no preconceptions and no identities that need to be held as barriers against what wants to come in.

When an old Zen master was asked about this "I don't know mind," he said, "Not knowing is most intimate." Since knowing gives us definition and control, it enables us to keep the world at arm's length. Having established our ideas and preferences about what is, we no longer have to bother to pay attention. Not knowing, on the other hand, leaves us vulnerable and free. It brings us very close to experience, unprotected and fully engaged. Not knowing, we merge with what confronts us. We let go of identity and evaluation and allow ourselves to surrender to amazement.

In retreats and especially in our mountain monastery, where it is so very quiet, I am often able to practice listening in this radical way. When the mind becomes quiet and free of schemes and strategies, it is a real pleasure—an astonishment—to hear the peep of a bird, the roar of the creek, the crunching of feet on the gravel path, or the clattering of dry leaves in the windswept branches. *Intimate*, with all its connotations of warmth and ease and pleasure and coziness and no need to prove or accomplish, is a good word for this experience. Sometimes in meditation I practice—and instruct others to practice—simply listening: sitting still, letting go of everything in the mind, and focusing intently on sound. Sometimes you hear the sound of your own heartbeat. And sometimes you hear the sound of your heartbeat and the sound of the wind or the stream as the same sound. Su Shih, the Song Dynasty Chinese poet, wrote soon after his enlightenment experience: "All night long I hear a hundred thousand scriptures in the sound of the mountain stream."

We all instinctively know how to listen in this way, and we don't have to be deep in the mountains to do it. There is no trick to simple listening. We just shut up, stop what we are doing, cock our ears, and listen. "*Shhh* . . . ," we say, and then, with a hush in our voice, ". . . *listen.*" The only problem is that we forget to do it, and the only way to remember is to keep coming back to this kind of listening over and over again, so that we begin to develop the habit.

So practice listening: turn off the radio, turn off the television, and just listen once in a while. Listen to traffic or work sounds. Listen to your own thoughts. And of course, listen to others. Start with people in your own family and set up special times, and special exercises, for listening. Make it a priority.

I think this profound kind of listening is the source of all inspiration and creativity. I imagine that sages of old—biblical prophets, shamans, poets, musicians, and artists—all tapped into this listening as the wellspring of their visions and insights. I know as a poet that my practice is almost entirely the practice of listening. I practice receptivity to the poem, to its shape and to its impulses. I don't write the poem. I let it write me.

There's a wonderful passage in the Surangama Sutra, an old Chinese Buddhist text, that describes the magical listening of Kuan Yin, the bodhisattva of compassion, whose representation sits on my office altar. Kuan Yin's practice is deep listening to the heart of the world. Through this practice, she "turns the mind around," and saves it from the suffering of outward grasping, allowing the stillness to emerge that understands that nothing is outside or inside and that nothing is incomplete or lacking. Through this profound practice of listening, Kuan Yin acquires various miraculous powers and grounds of self-confidence. She is able to hear all the cries of the world and to respond to each and every one of them with appropriate help. With her many hands and eyes she becomes a protector for the world—the world's helper and lover.

All of these wonderful consequences, however, derive from only one side of the practice of listening—the inspiring, beautiful side. It is also the easy side. Flowers and trees listen with this kind of purity, and we have to try to listen purely, too.

But in the human world there are complications. For better or worse, we have the capacity and the responsibility to exercise choice and action, to evaluate and to respond to what we hear. Although we need to be able to practice total receptivity in listening, we also have to do more than this. We cannot only be passive listeners. In the end, listening's completion is *negotiation*.

Conversation is a give-and-take. If we don't listen, we don't hear anything, and real conversation is over before it begins. We haven't taken anything in, and so we are just beaming our message at the other person.

But if we do take in what the other person is saying, this is just the beginning. Next we have to give something back—we have to respond. The key is to be willing to hold what you give and what you receive in balance, to be aware of and interested in both sides of the conversation, so that something dynamic occurs.

In our Zen community we have often set aside special times to work on listening and responding. After all, we have been living together fairly intimately, some of us for many years, and misunderstandings that harden into conflicts could be (and have been!) disastrous for us. So it is very practical and very necessary for us to learn to listen to each other. We have an annual listening retreat at our temples (separate from our meditation retreats) and we also offer occasional workshops or trainings in listening.

Gary Friedman, a longtime friend and neighbor, has helped our community enormously over the years to improve our capacity for listening. He is himself an exceptional listener and mediator who has trained thousands of attorneys in North America and in Europe in the fine art of listening. Gary teaches two key listening techniques that over the years have become part of our community process. They are simple and commonsensical, and once you learn them and experience their effectiveness, you will be amazed to realize that you have for so long failed to do something so obvious and so useful. He calls these techniques "looping" and "dipping."

"Looping" is shorthand for "closing the loop of communication." Communication is an exchange, a transfer of something from one mind to another. You have something in your mind, you put it into words that you address to me, and I receive your words and form in my mind an impression of what those words were meant to convey. Presumably, I now know what was in your mind. The loop of communication is closed once I really do have in my mind the impression you wanted to convey. In order for the loop of communication to be completed, however, it is necessary that I actually listen. If I don't actually hear what you have been trying to tell me (which is what usually happens) but instead have leapt to a conclusion or an assumption based on my own preconceptions, misunderstanding will snowball if the conversation proceeds along in this way. It is entirely possible that I will become quite upset with you for something you did not mean and did not say. And if I do, and if I react out of that upset, then it is likely that you *will* say or do something very shortly that really will upset me. And on it goes.

Looping is the technique of checking to making sure that the loop of communication has been completed. When I loop, I am making sure I really heard what you said. Looping slows down the conversation and gives us both the chance to see whether we are listening to each other accurately as we go along. Then, if we are going to disagree and get upset with each other (and of course we well might), at least we will be upset accurately, based on real differences of opinion rather than imagined or projected ones.

An exercise in looping works this way: you speak, I listen carefully. I do not interrupt or occupy myself with my own thoughts. I listen 100 percent. When you finish speaking, I repeat to you as closely and carefully as possible what I have just heard you say. I try to leave out all my interpretations, judgments, and reactions to what you have said and simply repeat it as straight as I can, as if I were a tape recorder. You then listen closely to my repeating your words (they need not and will not be exact, of course, but all the parts of what has been said, even the digressions, must be included), and you let me know whether what I have repeated is accurate and complete. If it is not, you don't complain. You simply fill in what I left out or correct my misapprehensions. Then I repeat back to you what you have just told me. When you are satisfied that I have heard you, then the loop of communication is closed and I can go on to reply to you. As Gary often tells us, a successful looping is your ticket to speak. In the communication exercise, you can't speak until you have demonstrated that you have really listened.

The practice of "dipping," Gary's second technique, has to do with listening to ourselves. The chief reason we don't listen to other people is that we're distracted. We're listening with only half our mind. With the other half we are busy talking to ourselves. As a result of this divided listening, we hear neither ourselves nor the other person. With looping, as we have just seen, we carefully listen to (and demonstrate that we have listened to) the other person. With dipping we listen just as carefully to ourselves.

To practice dipping in a conversation, take the time to *intentionally* stop listening to the other person (as opposed to distractedly forgetting to listen) and check in with yourself. Do you have a feeling, positive or negative, about what you are hearing? Do you have a feeling that is unrelated to what you are hearing, something that just popped into your mind for no reason, or that popped in as a result of what you have been hearing?

Of course, things are always popping into our minds during conversations and at other times. Generally we don't notice them, although they may exercise an enormous influence over what we say and how we react in conversation. If, for instance, I am upset about a conversation I had a short while ago with another person and am not quite aware of it, then certainly when you approach me with a problem you have with me, I am not going to be able to hear you too well. If I react with irritation and anger, you will think my reaction is entirely about you, and we will have a bad time of it. Or if your words have in fact upset me quite a bit and a powerful anger or fear or sorrow is arising in me, it is good for me to know this clearly and to realize that it will certainly be conditioning my own words in response to you. So I need to take a short time out to dip—to recognize that I am upset, perhaps to see why, and to take that into account.

In ordinary conversation you have to be able to dip from time to time without losing track of what is going on with the other person's words; this is not so easy, but it is possible to do once you get used to it. But when you are communicating explicitly using these techniques (which you can do, say, in an intentional group process, agreeing to use them all the time, or once in a while, when communication seems particularly problematic), you can say out loud that you want take a moment to check out how you are feeling.

Dipping may involve saying out loud how you feel. This can be very helpful. It can be extremely educational if the other person understands how his or her words have affected you or if he or she learns that something strong is going on in you that has nothing to do with his or her words. Most people imagine that their words are inconsequential, and it can be a shock to realize that their words can be effective and powerful, even if negatively so. But it is not always necessary for you to say out loud what you feel. It is only necessary that you yourself know.

When our community works with Gary in the context of a workshop, or when he comes to do a sort of "intervention" to help with communication between specific individuals who are having a hard time together, he often stops the conversation and asks one participant or the other to dip. Everyone just waits for a moment. Then Gary asks whether the person who has dipped would like to say what he or she is feeling. That person is free to say yes or no.

One of the most impressive demonstrations of these techniques I have ever experienced occurred during a nasty argument that my wife and I had. It was a rainy night after a long workweek, and we were on the highway in a huge traffic jam. We were en route to a friend's cabin where we were to spend the weekend discussing an important family decision. Neither one of us was quite sure how the other felt about the issue at hand, though of course we both had our preconceptions and fears. Ahead we could see an endless line of red taillights in front of us, and an endless line of yellow headlights coming toward us. The rain was steady and chilly, the road was unfamiliar, and we felt pressure to reach our destination before it got too late. All in all a fairly aggravating situation. In the midst of it we began talking about our impending decision. Immediately we got into a terrible fight. We are not particularly an arguing couple, but this time we really got into a mess together, our voices rising, our hearts thumping, the emotional pace inside the car picking up as the physical pace on the highway slowed. Finally I said, "Wait a minute, time out. Let's do some looping and dipping."

So we slowed down the conversation and began carefully looping each other. It was astonishing. The simple decision to loop—almost even before doing it—changed everything in my mind. When I began to repeat to my wife what I had just heard her say, I could hear in my mind the words I was so strongly reacting against. They were not the words she was saying—they were words I was projecting onto what she was saying, out of my own fears and desires and bad habit of assuming attitudes on her part that weren't necessarily there. It was all so clearly and strongly off-base—obviously not what she had been saying at all. Slowing down enough to see this, I began to listen to her, and then I could hear what she was saying. I could repeat her actual words back to her.

We did manage to work out our decision that weekend, and it wasn't easy. In fact, it was agonizing and took a great many hours of discussion. But I am certain that had we not taken the time to make sure we were really understanding each other accurately so that we could get down to what we actually did disagree about—rather than what we thought we disagreed about—making our decision would have been far more difficult, if not impossible.

Careful listening can produce harmony and agreement out of apparent disharmony and disagreement. But sometimes, as in this case, real listening, though it helps to calm things down and therefore to make things clearer, doesn't eliminate disagreement. It may simply clarify the disagreement.

I suppose that on an absolute level there is no such thing as disagreement. If my listening is total and deep, if I have entirely let go of myself and the whole world, if my receptive beginner's mind is perfect, then nothing I hear is ever too great a problem. Everything and anything is workable. I think it is good to appreciate things at this level. We seldom do, and it would be liberating to be able to do it, even if only for a moment.

But in the everyday world of negotiation and opposing interests, there will forever be disagreements involving emotions, principles, and contention over the distribution of love, power, or goods. The truth is that most of our disagreements are trivial. We would all be capable of seeing this if we could only listen to ourselves and others long enough to evaluate our disagreements—and especially to consider their cost to us. Some rational reflection would usually lead us to simply let go of a small disagreement that is causing a large grief. If we gave ourselves the chance, we would quickly realize that it just isn't worth it.

On the other hand, some disagreements are not trivial, and even on reflection we would not want to let go of them because they are important to us. We have no choice but to work them out. In such cases we need to clarify the disagreement so that we can separate its real root from the attendant overlay of emotion. Disagreements need to be negotiated, and successful negotiation certainly depends on clarity and calmness. Sometimes even with clarity and calmness solutions cannot be found, disagreements go on for a long time, and we have to bear with them and suffer through them until at last they have run their course. But even then we don't sit back and simply wait for the storms to clear (though there may be a time and a place for that, too). We keep on trying to negotiate, to listen, to understand, to consider our own views and the views of others, to work toward change, compromise, accommodation. It might take quite a while, sometimes even a lifetime or more, but we have to be willing to keep on doing these things, because listening is the road to eventual peace.

I am thinking of the deep and old conflicts between nations and peoples that are now—and seemingly always have been—rife throughout the world. There are also intractable conflicts in workplaces, in families, and among friends and lovers whose pain and sorrow can influence us for many years. Although it may take a long time to work out these conflicts, we can never afford not to try. It won't do to set them aside and just go on with things. We can never give up making an effort to listen.

Conversation is the culmination of listening. It includes everything I have been talking about—self-confidence, receptivity, give-and-take, even disagreement and conflict. Conversation is dialogue, real communication and communion through our words and our presence. Founded on deep listening, deep speech, and an honest self-awareness without too much fear or judgment, conversation is a way to connect with ourselves and with each other, to enter each other's lives and help each other heal.

What primarily keeps us feeling lonely and misunderstood—and fuels our hatreds and prejudices—is simply a lack of conversation. We all talk most of the day. We talk at work, at school, at home. But how much do we really say, and how often do our words get at what really matters to us?

Rabbi Nachman of Braslav, an eighteenth-century Hasidic rabbi, had a practice of holding conversation with God. He'd concentrate his mind and heart, grow quiet within himself, and then pour out his honest words to God, telling his troubles, his hopes, his fears, his aspirations. He considered this conversation to be the highest form of meditation and prayer. It healed him and gave him a way to go on. Other people pray in this way as well, bringing forth words from their souls out into the world in order to clear and release their hearts. Conversation between two people, if carried on with that amount of sincerity and confidence in themselves and in each other, can also be a form of prayer.

A crucially important element of my own spiritual practice is "practice interviews." Called in our tradition *dokusan* (literally, to meet yourself), these intimate meetings between teacher and student take place within a formal setting, often during meditation retreats, when both the student and I have had a chance to practice receptive deep listening on our meditation cushions. Out of the quiet and mindfulness that this provides, we come to meet each other, and in doing this each of us meets himself or herself—and everything else.

The English word *interview* describes it quite well: we "interview" each other, sharing our views together, mixing them until they merge, with a mutuality inspired by trust and openness. Since all of us are inevitably a mass of intersecting and conditioned viewpoints that come from our upbringing, our education, our experiences, our wounds, our desires, our joys, and our sorrows, we are communing with each other on an intimate basis when we interview each other, and thus freeing ourselves from the blindness that our views can so easily foster. Over the years I have come to appreciate these interviews and the range of what happens in them, and I feel fortunate to have such a practice in my life. I hold *dokusan* frequently, and I always look forward to it. No matter what kind of mood I have been in beforehand, I always leave the interview room with a sense of reverence and hope for the human condition. I have a great admiration for the wisdom of the ancients, who in creating this practice of interview, saw the transformative possibility of simple human communication.

Practice interviews take place in most Zen retreats, but for each student they represent only a small part of the retreat, which mainly takes place in silence. Interviews take place only between teacher and student—they do not take place between students. Thinking about this, and about the power and importance of conversation for spiritual practice, I began some years ago to experiment with a new kind of Zen retreat, one that isn't entirely silent. In these retreats we do much silent sitting practice, but there is also time to engage in conversation. With our ears cleared out by the sitting practice, and with some careful structures, we find that we are able to speak and listen to one another more deeply than is usually possible.

Our structure is this: in groups of three or four, each person is given the chance to speak uninterrupted for six or seven minutes. During this time the nonspeakers practice listening intently—not thinking about what they are going to say when it is their turn to speak, not evaluating what they are hearing, not allowing their minds to wander to other concerns, but simply listening as precisely and attentively as possible. After each person has had a chance to hold the floor in the surrounding space of the others' listening, dialogue and discussion begin.

Most of the retreats I do this way are for people who work in the world of business, which I don't know a thing about. I got into doing these retreats some years ago when I had a chance to attend a meeting of businesspeople. This was in the early 1990s, when many businesses were downsizing for the first time. Many employees were laid off, afraid of being laid off, or in a state of grief over all their coworkers who had just been laid off and the resulting extra work for them. I was dismayed as I listened to people speak of the heaviness and pain of their feelings—and of the fact that there was no place for them to go to discuss it. They couldn't discuss their feelings at work, and it was too difficult to do so at home, where families might be destabilized and upset by such talk. They were relieved to be able to commiserate at the meeting. Hearing all of this, I wondered out loud whether it would be of any benefit to hold a retreat at our temple for the purpose of sitting together in silence and then conversing about these things. Everyone was very enthusiastic, and the "Company Time" retreats began.

We have been doing these retreats now for some years, and they have moved beyond support group status. In an ongoing conversation about the possibility for spiritual practice in the workplace, we come together several times a year to sit silently and to talk. Through our conversations we are sharing and developing a vision and a community built on the notion that it is possible to be a fully feeling and aware individual at work, and that it is okay to admit this and to share it with our coworkers.

I offered one of my sitting-talking-listening retreats at the peace conference in Belfast, Northern Ireland, which I mentioned earlier. We practiced sitting, and then we practiced listening, this time using the techniques of looping and dipping. People's reactions to this practice were startling. They were genuinely shocked by several things. First, they exclaimed how wonderful it was to listen, and to be able to speak when someone else was actually listening. Many of them noted that although we were several days into the conference, which consisted of almost nothing but listening and speaking, this was the first time they had felt they had actually heard someone, and had been heard. Second, people noticed how difficult it was to listen with accuracy. Almost everyone found, after they had looped the speakers, that they had made numerous mistakes and misapprehensions and that they had left out or distorted whole sections of what had been said. People remarked that it was no wonder that the Protestants and the Catholics of Northern Ireland had such an impossible time getting along. How could they even begin to make peace if they literally couldn't hear what the other party was saying?

Another time I did the same exercise of listening and speaking at a short retreat I gave for employees of Yale University in New Haven, Connecticut. The various pairs of speakers went to different rooms to speak, and I roamed around to listen so that I could get a sense of what kind of experience the participants were having. In one group a man was speaking about how the exercise had gone for him. "I am a manager," he was saying, "and am fairly high up in the pecking order. So people listen when I talk. For years this has been the case: I talk, they listen. But today I discovered that even though they look as if they are listening, they actually aren't listening. I am not sure if, before today, I have ever actually been listened to by anyone. It feels great!"

Being heard does feel great. We all want to be listened to— we all need it. Many of us suffer terribly for lack of it. When you consider the problems of sexism, racism, ageism, classism, or homophobia, which have had tragic effects throughout the world, they really stem in large measure from the fact that people are not recognized and are not heard. Everyone wants and needs to be included in the human family, and being included means more than being equal under the law, more than having equal economic and social opportunity. It means being heard, truly heard.

During the time I spent in conversation with the four boys, I came to feel that adolescents, too, desperately need to be heard and seldom are. Their hearts full of the uncertainty that comes with shifting identity, they find it almost impossible to listen to themselves and to each other. They desperately need to be heard by adults, but they almost never are because adults are prejudiced against them. The truth is that adolescents have a bad reputation with adults, most of whom view them in their unruly awkwardness, moodiness, and exuberance, as alien, absolutely "other."

Think about how you feel when you see a group of adolescents approaching you on the street. Do you look at them with curiosity and interest? Do you move a bit closer to hear what they might be saying, to experience a little bit of their atmosphere? Or do you find yourself tensing up, bracing yourself for their approach, and trying to avoid them? Because what they have to say so often seems challenging, angry, or unclear, adolescents are the last people we want to listen to, and yet they are the ones who need our listening most. And since they represent the future for all of us, it is in our best interests to do that listening.

During my time with the four boys, in our many meetings that sometimes seemed fruitless and sometimes were delightful, I found that listening to adolescents is also listening to ourselves. Talking to them month after month about what it really means to grow up and joining them in their struggles with all the questions about living in our difficult time as an independent, responsible human being, I found that I was reliving these questions for myself, making them fresh, bringing them to life.

When I really did *listen*—which is to say, when I could overcome the temptation to advise them and share my wisdom and experience and instead could be with them in all their doubt and uncertainty—my own life was affected. Little by little it became impossible for me to coast along on the answers I had found out for myself in my own youth. They were fine answers and had stood me in good stead. But they were old answers, products of a person who no longer was and a world that no longer existed. Gradually I saw all of my old answers called into question. It was almost as if all those often laborious meetings with these four boys were waking me up in ways I needed to be waked up. It was providing me with the ground of doubt and questioning I needed at that time in my life to really grow up myself.

The practice of listening will always raise more questions than it answers. In this it is fertile soil for the development of true human maturity.

Four

PERSISTENCE

THESE FIRST SIX OR SEVEN MONTHS MEETING WITH THE BOYS were dramatic, with plenty of highs and lows. In the beginning there was the excitement of embarking on something brand-new. On their own, the boys had made a commitment to do something that felt special, even unique. But naturally the novelty of meeting with the Zen priest in his Zen room wore off after a few months. Still, there was enough genuineness in our being together, in the way that we spoke and listened to one another, to keep the meetings something that we all looked forward to and enjoyed. We had many great conversations that left a warm afterglow. But that, too, wore off as time went by and the boys seemed to return to more habitual ways of relating to me and to each other. After about six months we hit a bumpy patch.

Something was going on with the boys—with them as a group, and with each of them separately. I couldn't tell what it was. The dynamics between them were changing. Tony and Rashid, who had come into the group as close friends, seemed not to be so close any longer. Rashid was upset about something, and this distracted him so much that he seemed incapable of relating reasonably to anyone. Tony, for his part, was growing more sullen by the week. Sam continued to be diffident. His body language was eloquent: he shrank back from the others, literally leaning away from them, and he almost never spoke. Some meetings it seemed that he hardly even lifted his head to look at anyone. Meanwhile, James seemed more and more uncomfortable with something, maybe mostly with himself. Whenever he said anything—and he said a lot—you could hear him second-guessing himself. He seemed perpetually flustered and embarrassed. In short, all four of the boys were becoming normal adolescents.

One day Rashid came to our meeting in an extremely agitated state. He spent the first half of the time acting out disruptively. This was disturbing to all of us, and it was the first and only time I'd ever had to engage in a disciplinary conversation, taking him out of the room into the hallway to speak with him in private for a moment. Because of our practice of listening, and because, despite the ups and downs we had been experiencing, we'd hung in there with each other, a sense of trust had developed between us. I'm not sure we knew that until this day when, out there in the hallway, Rashid started to cry as he told me what was on his mind. We came back into the room and he told the others, too—about the marital troubles his parents were having, about the tension he felt in the household, about how that tension tied his stomach into knots so that he was having trouble sleeping at night and staying interested in school.

It was a relief finally to hear Rashid come out with all this. I had asked him repeatedly over the last month or so what was up with him, but he would never say. It was obvious that something was going on, and it was difficult to get through meeting after meeting with Rashid acting out the way he had been. But I kept my patience, for I knew that I couldn't force anything. I knew that we would hear about it when Rashid was ready to speak.

Persistence—the ability to hang in there with something difficult without turning away, to be willing to simply wait when waiting is what's called for—is not a throwaway virtue, and it is not simply a form of passivity. Persistence is a powerful and positive virtue that can be cultivated and developed. It's a key practice for nurturing all the qualities of maturity that we value: stability, responsibility, self-acceptance, a loving heart—all require that we persist with what we are up to, that we stick with it steadfastly, without glancing off or running away.

I have had a lot of experience with the practice of persistence, and I have needed it. I am naturally an impatient person, and when I was young I was given to great bouts of unbridled frustration at the way the world so often insisted on not cooperating with my needs and desires. The power of my anger was quite frightening, I think, to my parents, who were mild-mannered people. When I began Zen practice, I felt a good deal of frustration because the practice was so difficult. It was physically difficult to wake up early and sit long hours in meditation, especially during weeklong retreats and monastic training periods, which went on for months at a time without relief. But more than this, it was emotionally difficult, because it was impossible to be successful at it. The harder you tried, the worse it got, the further the goal receded from you. There's a koan about this. When the master is asked, "What is the Way?" he replies, "Everyday mind is the Way." The student says, "If everyday mind is already the Way, how can I aim for it?" The master replies, "If you aim for it, you will be going in exactly the opposite direction."

Patience wasn't my problem alone. Compared to most kinds of training and study, Zen practice really is frustrating. But this is part of the method: pressured by frustration, you have no choice but to develop persistence if you are going to continue. This is how it was for me. Besides being impatient, I am also quite stubborn, so far from discouraging me, the difficulty and frustration of Zen practice only made me more determined to go on.

Stubbornness and persistence are not the same thing. Stubbornness has a meanness to it, like a pit bull hanging on to a pants leg. It's reactive and often self-destructive (as it was in my case). Persistence, on the other hand, is not reactive or mean. It has a quality of faith and determination to continue, whether results are apparent or not. Persistence bears you up and helps you to move forward against the odds. In fact, with the practice of persistence, odds don't matter much one way or the other. Persistence doesn't wear you out by forcing you into a tight corner, as stubbornness does. Persistence provides some calmness in the face of adversity. It has been my job through the years of my Zen practice to massage my stubbornness, little by little, into persistence. I am still working on this.

In the shaping of our lives, we pay a fair amount of attention to skill and effort, to intelligence, talent, good looks, technique, training, education, and so on. But it seems to me that a primary virtue is the simple ability to be persistent with what you do, to not look for quick fixes or miracle cures, to be able to go on with a good feeling come what may.

The real beauty of persistence—and its true power, as the boys and I discovered in our time together—is that it eventually blossoms into trust. And trust is the secret ingredient, the magic of our lives. It's what makes all our relationships, including our relationship to ourselves, satisfying and in the end fruitful. Trust is always lovely and always touches us deeply, and its healing effects can last a lifetime.

A person who chooses to walk the path of maturity is a trusting and trustworthy person. He or she has learned, through clear observation over time, that there is no alternative to trusting what is, for to mistrust what is, is to reject our life experience, which is all we've got to build on, no matter how hard it may be. To take our places in this world we need to trust the world, ourselves, and each other this much.

The word *trust* comes from a Germanic and Old English complex of words that suggest firmness, reliability, steadfastness. The word *tree* comes from the same root words, and trees are the very image of solidity, faithfulness, and dignity. Cognate words include *truth* and *truce* and *pledge*. According to legend, Buddha's mother gave birth to him as she leaned against a tree. Buddha meditated under a tree, was enlightened under a tree, and died lying down between two trees. Buddhist meditators throughout the generations have been instructed to "sit at the foot of a tree" for meditation or to do walking meditation near trees. Simply to look at a tree mindfully, to stand under a tree with appreciation, or to stroll in the woods with a quiet heart can be wonderful spiritual practices. We need trees as trees for their own sake, of course, but also for ours: trees stand for the possibility of steadfastness and trust in our lives.

For most of us trust is difficult. We have experienced the unreliability of people and of the world at one time or another, in small and sometimes large ways. We know that there are no guarantees in life and that it is foolish to trust naively. If we do, we think, we will probably be betrayed, taken advantage of, made a fool of, lose out. Because we want to avoid and are quite frightened of those possibilities, we find trust risky. It seems much safer and more rational to be wary.

But the practice of persistence can shift this attitude. When you dedicate yourself to showing up, to coming back over and over again to a situation or relationship regardless of how it seems to be going, when you seem to be strengthened by frustration rather than frightened off by it, a serenity begins to set in. You see that producing or avoiding any particular outcome isn't really the point. Simply being there is the point. Trust is the point. If you keep on showing up long enough, trust will dawn in you—not trust that things will turn out a particular way, or that a person will give you what you want, but a bigger, wider trust, a calm feeling inside. A trust in what is. And a trust in yourself, confident that whatever happens, you will be able to make use of it somehow.

This special kind of trust born of persistence is truly remarkable when manifested in human relationships. Showing up, as the boys and I did at our mentoring meetings, week after week, month after month, making a practice of persistance, began to create the atmosphere of trust that gave Rashid enough confidence to begin finally to speak his mind, and his doing so, in that trusting atmosphere, was healing for us as well as for him. *Dedication, devotion, diligence*—these words could all be synonyms for the persistence I am talking about. Although they may seem like fairly prosaic virtues, they produce a power that is hard to match. Mature people know the sheer power of simply showing up.

A lot of what I have discovered about the transforming effects of persistence and how it leads to trust comes from my time as a high school teacher. I came to the profession later in life than most, and I did my student teaching at the local high school, in the town near the Zen Center where I lived. The school's demographics reflected the white, middle-class community in which it was located. But the school also served a smaller outlying African American community. The youngsters from that community were, on the whole, a fairly alienated population within the school.

Entering high school is a shock for any student. The social situation (you have only a few friends in a sea of new faces), the academic demands (chemistry?!), the knowledge that after high school you are going to be leaving home to go off to who knows where—all conspire to make the transition quite stressful. This ordinary difficulty was greatly compounded for the African American students, who had come from a predominantly black middle school.

The white school community—students, faculty, and administration—was liberal, fair-minded, and certainly not intentionally racist. But the community had very little understanding of and appreciation for what the African American students felt and how they saw the world. So it was easy to see why the African American students felt misunderstood and unseen. They kept to themselves and did their best just to get through. In fact, most of them didn't. Although the school targeted the African American students with good special programs of all sorts, the programs were always a bit off-putting to the students, and so were by and large ineffective.

I wanted to get to know the African American students better, so I decided to start a writing group, which I ran on a volunteer basis once a week. I recruited several students who said they were interested. But when the time came, only one or two students showed up—and many times no one came at all. It was disappointing. I would stand there in the empty classroom waiting (occasionally someone did come, maybe half an hour late for the forty-five-minute session) and digesting my feelings, trying to let go of my affront and disappointment—feelings that, of course, weren't helping. On days when no one at all showed up, I'd go out into the school yard. Often I'd see one or several of the writing group members hanging around there. When I'd ask them why they hadn't shown up, they would cheerfully give me some far-fetched excuse about what had happened. Yes, they'd be there next time. For sure. No problem. And they never were. I was fairly certain they were putting me on.

Still, I kept showing up. This was my practice of persistence. Maybe I was being foolish, but it's what I did. When no one showed up, I'd go out into the school yard and look for the students. They'd offer me yet another bizarre excuse, with assurances that they'd be there next time, and then we'd have a conversation.

After a while I realized that these conversations *were* the writing group. The truth is, they were pretty interesting, much more interesting than whatever writing exercise I'd have been able to cook up. I think the students also began to be impressed with my sheer doggedness and good humor. I knew perfectly well that their excuses were jokes at my expense and that their promises to come to the group next time were intentionally off-putting. But I never complained, and I really didn't mind. I just kept showing up.

One day the topic came around to racism. What about it? I was astonished at the sudden shift in mood: casual bantering turned to passionate, sharp, highly intelligent social criticism. The students eloquently analyzed American government, social mores, arts, culture, the school system, black culture and arts, black history and its implications. I got caught up in their enthusiasm. "Suppose we write about this," I said. "Suppose we write about racism. This stuff you're saying here, the way you're saying it, your experiences as black teenagers, not being actors or rap stars, not making it dramatic or special, but just the way it really is, in your own words. People need to hear from you. Suppose we write it up, tell the truth about how you see things. We could get a grant and publish a book about it so everyone can hear what you guys have to say."

This struck the students as exactly the thing to do.

It would be nice to say that after this my writing group was full at every meeting. But life is not so neat. The following week I think one or two, or maybe no one, showed up. We did start writing about racism. I had a method: we'd have a short conversation, develop a question about racism that we could write about, then sit around a round table together and all write about the question. (I wrote, too.) The practice was timed writing: don't lift your pencil until I say stop. There was some enthusiasm. But still, we poked along—until things turned around in the end because of one young man named Isaiah Howard.

Isaiah was a quiet but very impressive person. He was a star on the football team, a respected person among his peers. He had obvious integrity and real moral force. One day he showed up at the group, did the writing, wrote something that he thought was pretty good, and got the idea. He knew, I think, from my record of persistence above and beyond the call of duty—and even good sense—that I was trustworthy. He could see that I was not trying to impose anything on him or the others. He also saw that the project could be worthwhile, even important and useful. Then and there he committed himself to it and began to show up every week. He took on the practice of persistence. And because he showed up, three other kids showed up, and they practiced persistence, too, being as loyal and steady in the group as Isaiah was. One of the students, D'Ron, had a white mother. For him the group became a way of working out his racial identity.

Each week our times of writing, though short, were powerful and pleasurable. Sitting pretty close around the table, we could feel each other's concentration and energy. One of the group members, Ronnie Hughes, was always in trouble. He came from a family enmeshed in the drug culture and had a history of drug use and expulsion himself. He was incurably defiant and funny, with an uncontrollable big mouth. One week in the writing group Ronnie got inspired and wrote an elegant and energetic rap poem about how terrific it was to be black. We determined that we'd put the poem at the beginning of our book, as a kind of introduction.

Ronnie's poem was a high moment for all of us: it encouraged us to write more and better material. After many sessions we had quite a stack of it. Each week we'd add to it and admire the growing pile of pages. We were getting excited. As it turned out, we did receive a grant to self-publish the book. To get the grant the students had to make a personal presentation to the granting committee at its offices in the local civic center. They handled it masterfully.

To do the final edit of our book we went on a three-day retreat at the Zen Center and worked hard to pare down and streamline what we had. Within a few weeks production was complete, and our book entered the local bookstores under the title *Racism: What About It?*, with a wonderful photograph of the students on the cover. It was a smash success. For a long time I had to keep ordering more copies from the printer because it kept selling out. The youngsters were really proud of themselves and became famous in their community. Ronnie Hughes became a local celebrity and would stride around the school full of pride. One night we gave a reading at a local bookstore. The place was packed. There was one deranged lady heckler whom Ronnie handled with kindness, firmness, and consummate cool, managing to get us all out of what could have been a very difficult and embarrassing situation. I had never seen anything quite like it before.

To practice persistence you have to have a long-range view. If you expect to see results in a week or a month or a year, it's easy to get impatient. *I expected that something would happen by now,* you may think, *and it didn't. Why not, and who's to blame? And shouldn't I stop what I am doing now and go on to the next thing, which will surely bring me the rewards I am seeking?* When you expect a lot in a hurry, however, disappointment is guaranteed.

In our world short-term thinking is the norm. Our economy, our educational system, our social lives, even our personal goals are driven by short-term thinking. Sports teams rise and fall with this week's scores, businesses with the last quarter's profits or losses, and schools, influenced by business models, offer outcome-based education: by such and such a time such and such a student will be able to demonstrate such and such skills. If one looks at things exclusively through a short-term lens, it becomes impossible to consider questions of value and questions of maturity and inner ripeness, upon which, in the end, all lasting and worthwhile results depend. Such questions do not even compute on the short-term scale.

It's not that we shouldn't make immediate plans or try to achieve immediate goals. There is no way to live in a human world without doing this. We make appointments we plan to keep. We embark on projects we expect to complete. We set short-term goals we try to achieve. But we are relaxed and open-minded about the realization of our plans and the achievement of our goals. We recognize that there is always a very good chance that what we are aiming for will not come about. Despite all our good efforts, outcomes are never really predictable. They are simply not within our control. The appointment is canceled, or it turns out quite differently from what we expected. The project runs into an unforeseen snag. The goal can't be met, or it is met but has far different consequences than we had anticipated; sometimes there are no discernible consequences at all. Something that may have seemed initially to be bad turns out later to have good effects, or the good consequences we worked for turn out to have disastrous implications down the line.

As we come to see by careful observation over time, it is impossible to know what kind of results are being produced in the long run by our actions. Of course we try our best to plan and shape our actions. But we know that too intense a focus on short-term effects usually leads to disappointment and ineffective action in the end. The more flexible and open we are to what occurs, the better things will go in the long run.

The view of the bodhisattva—the enlightenment being who is working on his or her own maturity and whose goal is to aid others toward their maturity—is essentially a long-term view. The bodhisattva knows that short-term, results-driven planning doesn't work very well; instead, he remembers the "I don't know mind" that is open, flexible, and sensitive, moving easily with changing conditions. Paying attention to results, both long- and short-term, is practical and cannot be ignored. But results come and go—good results suddenly turn bad, or bad results suddenly turn good. Results don't measure anything. They are just rough indicators of what might be going on.

I have always lived my life trusting more to values and commitments than to results. Having faith in your values and commitments and remaining true to them, being courageous enough to act on them no matter what—being, in a word, persistent—will always lead you where you want to go. You come to trust this after a while.

The traditional Buddhist concept of karma has a lot of implications for thinking about short-term results and the long-term view. Although the analysis of karma is fairly complicated in Buddhist thought, its basic thrust is fairly simple: actions have consequences. Good actions have good consequences, bad actions have bad consequences. In any given moment of your life you are presented with a situation whose roots are in the past. This situation is a given. You cannot change it. But in the middle of this given situation you face a choice: What will you do? Will you be discouraged and impatient, emphasizing the worst of the situation, or will you, with persistence, make the effort to turn that situation toward the good for others and yourself?

No matter what your situation is, no matter how fortunate or dire it seems, this choice is always there, always staring you in the face in each moment of your life. It's inescapable. And each moment, whether you intend it or not, whether you make an effort or not, you always do inevitably make your choice. Consciously or unconsciously, every moment you are choosing your life, and that choice is always decisive, never trivial. Your choices always have important consequences for the future, whether you can see them immediately or not.

Recognizing the importance of your choices helps you to cultivate the attitude necessary for the practice of persistence. Yes, there is much in your life that you simply cannot change and need to accept, without complaint. What has happened really has happened, and it can't be undone. The person you are, the social and intellectual forces that have shaped your attitudes—these are what they are. And yet, given the situation you find yourself in, at any moment you have the power, and the obligation, to choose how you will act. You can choose to act for the good or not, and your action one way or the other will definitely be effective in the long run, even though you may not yet be able to see how. If you look at things like this, you will quite naturally persist in your wise action because you are certain that what you are doing is for the good, regardless of the short-term results.

You don't need to take anyone's word on this claim. If you study your intimate experience carefully, you will see for yourself that it is true. For example, when you indulge your natural impulse to be angry or blaming, you become agitated and unhappy, and those with whom you are angry become enemies, making your life uncomfortable. If, on the other hand, you try your best to let go of anger or blaming, then your heart is more at ease and the person who was the object of your anger is either neutral to you or even friendly. It is true that in the short term your anger may help you to win your point. But in the long term, if you persist in letting go of anger and blaming, your happiness will increase and your relationships will become more positive. Winning your point will give you only short-term satisfaction, to be followed later by more battles, more anxiety, and more chances to lose.

If you test this out repeatedly, you will become convinced—as I have through much bitter and sweet experience—that long-term confidence in the power of goodness is never misplaced. With that confidence you won't focus so much on short-term gains because you will know for certain that a long-range commitment to the good produces much stronger gains in the end.

Human conduct in this world is often very discouraging and it would make sense that any of us would feel impotent and dismayed by it. After all, what can any one person do? If even the leaders of nations, who supposedly have their hands on the world's tiller, seem to be powerless to make things better, what are we ordinary people to do? But when you see the power of persistence and the certainty of long-term good results flowing inevitably from good actions, no matter how small and personal those actions may be, you do feel that what you do matters and makes a difference in this world. Drops make brooks that flow on eventually as rivers and oceans—and this is the only way rivers and oceans are made.

If you reflect on any personal quality you might be trying to cultivate, you begin to realize that developing that quality depends on working with its opposite. If you want to cultivate love, you have to work to overcome hatred and indifference; if you want to be strong, you have to work with what is weak within yourself in order to become stronger. And so it makes sense that the cultivation of the practice of persistence mostly has to do with studying and working with frustration, because frustration is the main obstacle to persistence.

Frustration isn't entirely bad, of course. If you are stubborn like me, frustration can spur you on. And even if you aren't stubborn, frustration is useful because it can motivate you to change a situation that should be changed. When you get frustrated enough, you look at conditions, discover what can be adjusted and fixed, and then roll up your sleeves and do what it takes to improve things.

It's nice when it's possible to improve things, but unfortunately it sometimes isn't. Often we are frustrated by conditions that can't be changed, or can be changed only at tremendous cost. We're frustrated with other people whose behavior is impervious to our correction, with illnesses that can't be cured, with losses that can't be prevented, with terrible social conditions that persist, or with emotions that arise in us that are just going to be there no matter what we try to do about them. Such frustration can be overwhelming and may easily escalate into anger, despair, or some other form of acute anxiety or shutting down—insomnia, compulsive behavior, addiction.

There's nothing good about being overcome with frustration; it is entirely counterproductive. There is much wisdom in the serenity prayer of Alcoholics Anonymous: "God grant me the serenity to accept the things I cannot change, the courage to change the things I can, and the wisdom to know the difference." No matter how justified our anger over our frustrations seems to be, no matter how convincing our despair, it is obvious that anger and despair do us no good at all.

Persistence, on the other hand, is always helpful. Persistence is not gritting your teeth and toughing it out. It's not brute endurance, or stubbornness. Persistence—which could also be called endurance, forbearance, patience—is the positive quality of calmly and steadily sticking to your goal for as long as you see that you can. If your initial commitment to your goal was good, then being able to follow through is good, too. Even if you never reach your goal, a calm and persistent effort will have made your experience much more pleasant and worthwhile than frustration. Persistence is its own reward. Even if you give up your goal in midstream, it is better to make that decision with the calm mind of persistence than with the confused mind that is overcome with frustration and quits in disgust, weakened for the next thing that comes along. If you have to change course, it is better to do so with the feeling that you have learned something you can build on, even if you have been defeated in what you tried to accomplish.

In the Zen tradition there's a story that's often told about this kind of persistence, this calm and peaceful abiding with an impossible situation until something shifts. The story is usually attributed to Hakuin, an eighteenth-century Japanese Zen master. Once a young girl of the village became pregnant out of wedlock. When her parents asked her who the culprit was, she said it was Hakuin, the old priest on the hilltop. The parents were outraged, and when the child was born, they whisked it off to the temple in a huff, demanding that Hakuin take the child in. "Here is your doing," they told him. "Now you deal with it." And off they went. "Oh, is that so?" Hakuin said, accepting the warm bundle.

A year or so later the girl, overcome with remorse, finally admitted to her parents that she had lied. The father was not Hakuin at all, but a young man of the village whose parents were very strict and who would surely disown their son if they knew the truth. The girl's parents, on hearing this, were mortified and again raced up the hill to the temple in a panic of shame and guilt. Bringing gifts and offerings, they bowed deeply to Hakuin in apology and took the child back. "You are such a good priest not to have said anything, to have accepted our terrible words with such composure." "Oh, is that so?" the old priest replied. Hakuin's practice of persistence, his forbearance with conditions no matter what they brought, was so strong that he was affected by neither praise nor blame.

One very effective way to practice with frustration is to make a detailed study of it just at the moment when you find yourself in its grip. Trying not to be frustrated when you are is just piling more frustration on top of your frustration. So why not instead look at it close up? When you do, you will notice that when frustration arises, the first thing you naturally do is look for someone or something to blame—even if that someone is yourself. But as soon as you do that, you are actually increasing your frustration, because you are leaping over your actual experience of frustration—futilely trying to avoid it, in effect—by focusing your energies on the object of your blame. The pile of frustration is always too high, however, to leap over. You only fall back in, over and over again.

Blaming is useless. It is a smokescreen, a blind, a weight that drags you down and doesn't get you anywhere. It is important to notice this as soon as you are frustrated and start blaming. Catch yourself. (This takes practice—you have to be quick.) Then focus instead on observing the actual feeling of frustration.

What does frustration feel like? Does your breathing tighten? Do your shoulders tense up, or does your face get red and hot? Do you clench your teeth? Your fists? What thoughts fly into your mind? Are there memories that come up? Visual images? What is frustration really like?

Oddly, if you accept frustration as frustration and study it without trying to relieve it by blaming or becoming angry, it will not overcome you. Instead, it will dissipate fairly quickly, or at least more quickly. You will simply digest it naturally.

Every human being already has a degree of persistence: we need some persistence just to stay alive, to hold down a job, to keep a human relationship functioning. All of us show up for our lives to some extent. We are all more patient and forbearing than we know, and we should recognize this and congratulate ourselves for it. We don't need to create the quality of persistence out of nothing. Rather, we need to expand and strengthen the persistence that is already there. Cultivating persistence takes persistence.

Let's say that now you have studied frustration and you are clear that you can indeed work with it. You have seen that by not indulging frustration as you have previously done you can replace it little by little with calmness and persistence. At this point, when frustration arises, you may no longer be seeing it as something to be avoided at all costs but as a challenge, an opportunity, almost as something to look forward to! You can immediately turn toward it, stop what you are doing, and start consciously breathing. It might help to smile on purpose or to relax the muscles in your face or shoulders. One Zen master I studied with told me that when he was frustrated and didn't know what to do, he would close his eyes and imagine the waves breaking gently on the beach on the Japan Sea where he grew up. Let the frustration wash through you and fall away like those waves, then feel the calmness arise. This is really not so different from the old saw about counting to ten when you are angry. If you have the presence of mind to start counting with one, you will have a lot more presence of mind by the time you get to ten.

You have to work on this with very small things until you get better at it. View every little frustration, every little daily setback, as another chance to reduce your bondage to frustration and strengthen your persistence muscle. Pick one: getting cut off in traffic, forgetting where you put your keys, walking out of the grocery store and realizing that you forgot to get the one important item you went in for. If you can develop your skill with small things, after a while it becomes possible to use it with major frustrations. The more you practice, the better you get at it. You catch your frustration sooner and turn it into persistence more easily and more frequently, all the way up to the point at which frustration hardly arises at all. Instead, a general spirit of persistence comes up fairly consistently with whatever you do.

Don't think about progress or results, though. To stay with the practice of persistence you can't be occupied with progress or results. That would be counterproductive. If you do see results, wonderful, but it is good not to be too confident about them. The truth is that it is very difficult to have a positive attitude of persistence with the fundamental frustrations of life: everything we set up will fall down, and we eventually lose our family and friends, our bodies and minds, to death. Zen practice focuses on persistence at this level. Zen practice is mostly the practice of failure.

Practicing failure, total failure, is the ultimate practice of persistence. In Zen practice we come back over and over again to this point: right now, just the way we are, with all our problems, with all the built-in frustrations that come from loss and impermanence and the final vanity of everything human, we are also perfect and everything in the world is complete. The only thing necessary is to embrace this point.

Of course we can't do it. We always fall to one side or the other, either crying over our problems or, stupidly, thinking in a moment of transcendence that we are beyond all problems. Many of the Zen stories turn on this point: how to see any failure as *absolute* failure, beyond any idea of success or failure. An old Zen master used to say, "Whether you're right or wrong, still I'll give you thirty blows!"

Contemporary Zen is generally more gentle than this, at least in the West, but practitioners nevertheless go through a psychological impasse with failure. If the practice group and the teacher treat this impasse with kindness and respect, it can be very useful, and ultimately very strengthening. You have the inner experience so many times of being wrong, of failing to grasp life's fundamental point, of getting (metaphorically at least) those thirty blows whichever way you turn. But finally you see: it's so simple! It's just myself as I am, letting go of all ideas of gaining or losing. There are no mistakes, no mistakes at all, there's only what happens—what has happened, what is happening, and what will happen. Life is only life. It's always a little messy. But that's fine. That's what being human is all about. It's trusting your life in an ultimate way, trusting your own ultimate goodness and the goodness of the world that surrounds you, the world that is you and you are it.

Finding this sort of trust in yourself is not a solo endeavor. While it may be true that all of us have to find wholeness within ourselves, without expecting someone else to give it to us or to complete us in some way, nevertheless I have found—and much spiritual literature corroborates—that it takes another person, or probably several others, to help us to find this out. Human relationships provide the magic, the catalyst, we need to come to a true self-trusting that will water the seed of true maturity in our lives. This is what I found in the years I spent with the boys' mentoring group, and it's what I found with my Zen teachers and students, with my parents, with my family, and with friends. We touch and awaken each other, not so much in conscious ways—in ways we can figure out and produce at will—but just by persisting with each other, just by hanging in and being together.

Zen literature often uses the metaphor of a chick breaking out of an egg to describe the way in which trust nurtures and aids our maturing process. When the chick intuitively senses that the time is right, she begins to peck on the shell from the inside, gently at first, then with more and more force. This pecking is necessary, but it is not sufficient. Outside the shell the mother hen, seeing the chick pecking from inside, also begins to peck. With perfect trust and sensitivity their pecking is perfectly timed; the shell breaks and the chick emerges. In the emerging of the chick there is only blossoming, only life reaching its proper fullness. Although there is pecking from the outside and pecking from the inside, the experience is just one pecking, without boundary. A Zen master wrote a poem about it:

The chick breaks out, the mother hen breaks in.

When the chick awakens there's no shell.

Chick and hen both forgotten,

Response to circumstances is unerring.

On the same path, chanting in harmony,

Through the marvelous mystery, walking alone.

Five

CONNECTION

ONE DAY RASHID WALKED INTO MY STUDY FOR OUR MEETING with a completely different attitude. It was unmistakable. He carried himself differently—he walked slowly, and with dignity. Instead of hurling himself down on his seat, as he usually did, he sat down with gravity. As soon as we were all assembled and settled, he announced, "My parents separated over the weekend. My mom moved to an apartment downtown." He seemed relieved. The worst had finally happened.

Rashid wanted to talk about it, and he did, without pause, for over an hour. He talked about how the fear that had covered the unspoken feelings in his household had been like a hot iron rod in his body all through this time; about how much pressure he'd felt in everything he did, as though his words and deeds could bring his parents closer together or drive them further apart; about how angry this made him with his parents, with himself, with the world; about how crazy he had felt; about how much he had not realized what was going on, and then when he did, how much he didn't understand about how bad it was; about how trying not to think about it or talk about it had made it much worse; and about how now that what he had feared most had finally happened, as it had happened to so many of his friends and classmates, he knew he'd be able to deal with it.

For a long time, he said, he'd held a grudge against his parents for what they were unknowingly doing to him and to each other. Their problems were simple. They just had to stop being so stubborn, so headstrong, so oblivious to each other. He could see it—why couldn't they? Why did they have to make such a mess and then spread the mess to him and his brother? But now that it had finally happened and he could see their suffering, their confusion, their grief, he could understand that they couldn't help it. They were caught in their own traps and couldn't get out of them. Now that he saw how hard it was for them, he could forgive them. Now that he knew it wasn't really their fault, he could support his mother in her anger and frustration and his father in his bewilderment and sorrow. Now he knew that what happened wasn't his fault, but also that he could make it better, easier, because he could forgive. Rashid told us how much it meant to him that our meetings had continued, and that he had a place where he could say all that he was saying today, and that others would listen without trying to give him advice.

As I sat taking in Rashid's torrent of eloquence and wisdom, I began to appreciate again the power of human pain. So much of what motivates us in our lives is the avoidance of pain, at any cost. How often we distract ourselves, run away, strategize solutions that never work out, or just decide without really deciding not to take notice. But as I was now hearing from Rashid plainly, pain can never really be ignored or avoided. And when pain is confronted, it has the power to open us up—if it doesn't break us apart. It has the power to inspire us, as it had Rashid, to wisdom, forgiveness, and compassion. Nothing connects us more to life, to ourselves, and to each other than our unavoidable human suffering. This connection to the reality of our own lives that we make only through our own pain is the seed of our maturity. Although we can prepare the ground for growth through listening and persistence, it is only when we meet the suffering that inevitably arises in our lives that we are finally able to begin the real work of growing up.

In early Buddhism the focus on suffering was very clear. "I teach suffering and the end of suffering," Buddha often said in the earliest scriptures when asked to describe the essence of his doctrine. The whole of the Buddhist path was designed with this in mind—to see suffering for what it is, and then to live in such a way that suffering is not only reduced but entirely put aside. Nirvana, the path's goal, was said to be "cool," "extinguished," like a candle flame blown out. Buddhas were beings who had so completely quelled the restless energy of their desire and longing that they were now living their final life. After this present life, they would find total peace and would not return, as the rest of us do, to this world of strife and confusion again and again.

But with the emergence of the bodhisattva path in Mahayana Buddhism some centuries after the Buddha's lifetime, the passion for saving others through compassion became so strong that the path's goal changed drastically. Rather than working to end suffering once and for all so that there would be no more coming back into life through future rebirths, the bodhisattva worked to develop a compassion so powerful that it would cause him or her to return to life again and again— not to suffer fruitlessly and repeatedly but to suffer gladly and purposefully in order to benefit others. Rather than trying to end suffering, the bodhisattva made heroic efforts to absorb his or her own suffering and that of others and through that suffering to connect to life at the deepest possible level. In the Western Judeo-Christian tradition there is also this sense of the nobility and power of accepting suffering as the way to connect with our lives. The story of the Jewish people's enslavement in and liberation from Egypt is a story of redemption through suffering, as is the passion of Jesus, who suffers for and with all creatures.

Rashid had been suffering for some time, silently and without much awareness of what was going on. But now, his crisis coming to a head, his very suffering had suddenly become his path through it. Connecting to his own pain, he could see his parents' pain, and this enabled him to know them as he had never known them before. Before his parents' marital problems had happened—before the tension, the uncertainty, and now the separation—Rashid had simply taken his parents for granted. They were just there. Mom and Dad. As they had always been. Parental archetypes perhaps, problems for him in many ways, part of his story, but not really people on their own, in their own right. But now, with all that had been happening and all that he had been feeling, he began to notice what his parents were really like. They were both stubborn, each in a different way. His mother was quiet, and yet indomitable. His father was aggressive, and yet passive. Rashid didn't describe them this way, but he saw them quite astutely (and much more accurately than I could have despite the fact that I had known them for many years). And unlikely as this is, he saw them in their fullness—what was good about them as well as what was bad—and he saw them widely, with compassion and forgiveness.

Because of Rashid's experience, the other boys also began to take stock of their parents. They, too, had had the normal teenage view of their parents as overly protective, a little dense, a little dim. But beyond this, they also gradually came to see, through our discussions (which at this point I directed, quite naturally, toward the issue of parents), that their parents were both good people and limited people, as all people are. And like Rashid, they began to have a feeling of forgiveness toward them.

Forgiving our parents is an important step in the direction of maturity. It is astonishing how many people fail to take this step, choosing to remain, in effect, adolescents throughout their lives. Even into old age, many people maintain the same wounded, angry, or disappointed relationships with their parents that they formed when they were young. People I know who are like this say that they can't help it. Their parents are extremely difficult people, they say, and getting worse with age. They are certain that it is impossible to make peace with their parents and overcome the old hurts because their parents have constantly reopened the old wounds with each new encounter over the years.

I am sure my friends know what they are talking about. I have no doubt that these parents are just as impossible as their children say they are. (I have met some of these parents and can corroborate this!) And yet, although my friends may be quite right in their assessments, I disagree with their conclusions. Peacemaking never depends on the other person. Peace is made in our own hearts, and nowhere else. If negotiations and changes are to be made outside ourselves, these proceed (at least ideally) only after we have made peace within ourselves. If we are fortunate enough to have our parents' cooperation in the peacemaking effort, so much the better. But if not, the work goes on anyway.

Throughout the years of my spiritual practice I have met many people who thought that a serious engagement with spiritual practice could be a substitute for all this messy work. Taking up a lifestyle radically different from the one they grew up with and spending many long hours in meditation or prayer, they thought, would help them transcend the family wounds that had brought them to their practice in the first place. But eventually their spiritual practice, when they actually paid attention to it (and not everyone does—it is possible to be half-asleep in our practice), and whether they liked it or not, brought them back to their family wounds vividly enough that they had to deal with them. Sometimes they did this through psychotherapy, sometimes through dialogue with their families, sometimes through relationships with their spiritual teachers, and sometimes simply on the meditation cushion. Although we all have a tremendous capacity for self-deception and avoidance, the meditation cushion generally works against it. Sitting peacefully in a retreat one day, you may well be blindsided by a rush of feelings about your parents you never expected or knew were there.

The truth is that no matter what kind of upbringing we have had, whether we were raised by saintly parents full of loving kindness and wise in the ways of child-rearing or by parents who were just the opposite, all of us were hurt in our early years to some extent, and so all of us have some forgiveness work to do with our parents. Beyond the inevitable mistakes they made, there is the hurt and humiliation that life itself brings to all of us. Every child has been thwarted, every child has been terrified, every child has been turned back sometime when he desperately wanted to plunge ahead. Growing up always involves much humiliation and disappointment as those early feelings of omnipotence and promise gradually yield to the reality that the world is full of insurmountable obstacles, many in the shape of other people who may be stronger, smarter, better-looking, better educated, and more skillful than we are. Although from a rational point of view this reality may have nothing to do with our parents, from the child's imaginative and symbolic perspective all of life seems to be connected to them, to swirl around our memory of them or our relationship to them, like a troubling nimbus. The vulnerable child we all have been both absolutely loves and absolutely fears the all-powerful, all-wise parent who inevitably betrays the child's trust sometimes with an angry look, a cross word, or a threatening gesture, whether real or imagined.

I am sure that we all reach adulthood with a need to forgive our parents simply for being who they are or were. Many of us never do forgive them. Although our adolescent anger may subside, we go on for a long time harboring a heavy weight of guilt and occlusion in relation to our parents, a weight that we feel in our own living as a blockage of energy or love. So whether or not we are interested in making peace with our parents for their sake, we need to do it for our own.

I have a friend who is a geriatric psychotherapist. She runs groups for people who are over eighty years old. She tells me that the number-one topic in most of her groups is parents. Amazingly, the octogenarians are still chewing on childhood stuff, so many decades after their parents have left this world.

These knotty feelings focused on our parents apparently are much more powerful within the Western psyche than in the psyches of people from traditional Eastern cultures. There is a commonplace imaginative practice in Tibetan Buddhism that is used to help students generate compassion: they are asked to imagine that all beings are their mother—as if, in some distant past life, all beings actually had been their mother. The idea is that since all people naturally feel that there is nothing in this world more pure and more wonderful than a mother's love, imagining beings as our mothers will make us feel a strong and positive connection to them. But I have never attended any sort of meeting in the West in which this practice was given without hearing a few people in the audience say (what probably many more are also feeling), "Regard all beings as my mother to generate loving kindness! You must be joking! You have never met my mother. She is controlling and needy and absolutely impossible!"

Because I know how strong and pivotal our need is to forgive our parents, I created my own version of a traditional Buddhist loving kindness meditation. In one part of the practice, students visualize each of their parents in turn, and then repeat these phrases, as sincerely as they can: "May he (or she) be happy. May he (or she) be content with himself (herself). May his (or her) heart be open." This turns out to be a fairly tough practice. Most people find that when they try to send out these loving wishes for their parents, much ambivalence comes up. They often, though certainly not always, have a reservoir of love and positive feeling to bring to this practice, but just as often negative feelings arise, sometimes in relation to the parents but quite often in relation to themselves. It seems as if buried deep below our hurt feelings about our parents are hurt feelings about ourselves—such as guilt for having had so much antipathy toward those we are supposed to love, or self-hate derived from an unconscious identification with a parent we have rejected. Such feelings are complicated and differ from person to person. But observing people do this practice over the years has convinced me of the deep significance of our feelings for our parents.

Another practice that I have taught and often done myself is the practice of imagining our parents as children. I see my father as a skinny little boy. I see my mother as a frightened little girl. I imagine the clothes they are wearing, the places they are growing up in. It is likely that this little boy and this little girl have often been hurt, confused, upset, or utterly despairing. I see my father and mother as adolescents. Probably they looked at their parents with the same mixture of love and dismay, guilt and confusion, bitterness and respect, that I felt as an adolescent when I looked at them. Just as I struggled with them, they struggled with their parents. Certainly the way they related to me as a child had a lot to do with the way their parents related to them. And their parents had learned from their own parents, on and on into the distant past. There isn't anything I can do to change all that, but simply by appreciating it, vividly and visually in my mind's eye, I can forgive my parents for who they were and what they did. Maybe I have made the same mistakes with my own children that they did with me. Or maybe I have made other mistakes.

I have found that if people stay with this kind of practice without avoiding the complexities of the feelings that inevitably arise, but just allowing those complexities to come without trying to fix them and without giving in to resistance and avoidance, they eventually experience a moment of forgiveness, a moment of liberation from old feelings. And even, finally, some gratitude.

In the end our maturity demands that in accepting our parents we find a way to be grateful to them, no matter how terrible a job they may have done with us. To come to this acceptance and gratitude for our parents is to accept and be grateful for the lives we have lived. Although it may take a lifetime's work, and although even then we may not complete the job, to accept our parents with gratitude is to accept the world as it actually is and to understand its suffering and confusion with a wide wisdom. If we can forgive our parents for being who they are and understand the conditions that caused them to be the way they were, we will have a measure of peace in our own lives.

Although I have been arguing that we need to spend a long time working with our feelings about our parents—until we eventually reach the point of appreciation—in the end our growth demands that in some deep, inner sense we leave our parents behind. The myth of the Buddha's life has something to tell us about this aspect of working with our feelings about our parents. The prince Siddhartha (Buddha's name before his awakening experience) was a talented and skillful young man who enjoyed a happy life in the palace. He got along well with his family and was destined to succeed his father as king. Siddhartha's father was quite protective of his son. Hoping somehow, as all good parents do, to accomplish the impossible feat of shielding his son from the world's harshness, he tried to keep Siddhartha always near the palace, where life was pleasant and things went well. Of course this restriction could not hold. Siddhartha was after all a young man—he would naturally go exploring. He sneaked out of the palace grounds several times to see what the world was really like and was dismayed to discover the shocking truth about the human condition: suffering, old age, sickness, and death were inevitable for all.

In those days in India it was quite common to become a religious seeker in the face of such hard facts, and Siddhartha decided to undertake that life. Since this intention went counter to the wishes of his parents, he had to leave his family secretly in the middle of the night, without warning and without looking back. Later, as an enlightened sage, he began a new religious order of "homeless ones" who were required to leave their families entirely behind. When he eventually returned to his home territory on one of his many journeys, he was reunited with his parents, not as their son but as the

Awakened One, the World Honored One, the Buddha. Deeply moved, Buddha's father became a devoted lay follower, and his stepmother, who had raised him after his mother died in childbirth, became, poignantly and after much struggle, the first Buddhist nun.

Whether we like it or not, our parents play an integral part in our path toward maturity. They loom large in our psychic lives, giving us all the trouble and resistance we need, whether they intend to or not. Insofar as they have caused us suffering and we can connect to that suffering as part of our life's wounds and forgive them, they have also helped us. And yet, once we have connected to our own pain and the unique reality of our own lives—and thus truly begun our journey toward maturity—there is almost nothing our parents can do for us. The work of taking our places is our own work, never theirs. Like the Buddha, we must leave, spiritually if not physically, in the middle of the night. Our parents, good or bad, alive or dead, are going to do whatever they do and be whoever they are. We can't help that or change it one way or the other. But no matter what they do or don't do, what they are or are not, our path lies ahead, and it must go through and beyond our parents. Somehow we have to engage in a transformative struggle with our parents—or at least with the archetypal parents that exist in our minds. The struggle may be (though it need not be) painful and difficult and full of bitterness and misunderstanding. In fact, if we are aware of what is going on and understand the struggle as our own inner process that includes our parents, not as a political battle with our parents for control (as we may have viewed it in our adolescence), we can minimize the difficulty and the damage. Buddha's break with his parents was decisive, drastic, dramatic, and total. Ours is probably more gradual and internal. But either way, we, too, must be home leavers—and then, like

Buddha, we can eventually become returners, giving our parents good teachings for their own journeys toward the end of their lives.

These days I have many friends whose children are going off to college. There is a mixture of sadness and relief for them as they watch their children leave. I remember when I went off to college. I was one of the few in my high school graduating class who went to school out of state, and I viewed it as a tremendous adventure. My parents took me there and dropped me off at my dorm on a sunny fall day with all my bags. I couldn't wait for them to leave, and I do not remember experiencing anything more than a brief moment of sadness when they did go. By contrast, the day our first twin left home for college was one of the saddest days of my life—about as emotionally powerful for me as the day he was born. He was leaving to attend a very tiny college in the high California desert, and all four of us drove him there. The trip was absolutely terrible: driving there, depositing him in his room, camping out overnight, leaving the next morning. I will never forget the feeling of that day, especially waving good-bye to him and driving down that narrow dirt road away from the campus, watching him standing there getting smaller and smaller in the rearview mirror, continuously waving.

That's how it always goes. The Buddha once said, pointing out the obvious (as religious sages so often do), that all meeting ends in parting. If you can accept the truth of this and digest it, you will begin to realize that all your relationships are precious, for each one has taught you something unique that you could not have learned in any other way. Each of our relationships ought to be handled like a delicate gem, with full respect for its particular beauty.

Martin Buber tells a Hasidic tale that beautifully expresses this poignancy of human relationships. It is in the form of a commentary, given by Rabbi Barukh on a line in the 119th Psalm: "I am a sojourner on the earth; hide not thy commandments from me." Concerning this verse the great rabbi said: "He whom life drives into exile and who comes to a land alien to him has nothing in common with the people there and not a soul he can talk to. But if a second stranger appears, even though he may come from quite a different place, the two can confide in each other, and live together henceforth, and cherish each other. And had they not both been strangers, they would never have known such close companionship."

As close as we are to our parents, for good and ill they are strangers to us, like everyone we encounter in this world. For at the deepest levels of the heart none of us really understands other people or the world. We are all strangers here, gathered from other realms to make our destiny together. Each of us struggles to belong, to feel comfortable, to claim our own place. Such struggles are the journey of a lifetime. In this alien situation, as the rabbi says, it is a great comfort to meet and recognize another stranger, someone who knows our struggle, who appreciates our pain, because he or she is going through the same thing. Our parents are the first such strangers we encounter in this world.

Working to forgive our parents for being who they are usually brings into view the fact that we also need to forgive ourselves for being ourselves. It is truly staggering to recognize the extent to which most of us harbor serious grievances against ourselves. We are annoyed with ourselves in a million ways—we don't like our looks, our talents, our skills, our attitudes. As difficult as it may be to forgive our parents, it is even more difficult to forgive ourselves. Probably the latter depends on the former, or at least goes hand in hand with it. Our grievances against ourselves—our disappointment, anger, frustration, and dismay at our limitations and character flaws—are so deeply ingrained that most of the time we aren't even aware of them. They seem simply to *be* us, the wound that is our self. I have always considered it the pinnacle of the spiritual life when we can simply allow ourselves to be who we are, forgiving ourselves for all our failures to live up to our ideals and expectations. To see that who we are is a gift and a path forward, not a mistake.

Unlike the Buddha, who is depicted in the texts as a perfect human being, the Zen masters of old were rough, pungent characters with many foibles. Paintings of them show scraggly beards, scowls, and stooped shoulders, not glowing, smiling beatific countenances. Despite their many imperfections, the Zen masters didn't rail against themselves, trying desperately to become someone else. Instead, they embraced the way they were, taking on joyfully the task of being themselves and acting spontaneously and confidently. They seemed to celebrate themselves. Their long practice on their meditation cushions showed them the shape of essential human suffering as it had manifested in their own lives, and they came to accept that, affirm it, and make use of it. To really take our places in this world we need to forgive ourselves and accept ourselves. Without self-forgiveness and self-acceptance we are always at best slightly embarrassed about who we are, and at worst tortured.

If the key to forgiveness of self and others is connecting to our own suffering, you might be thinking, *I have been aware of my suffering for a long time, and it hasn't made me forgive myself or others. Aren't we all acutely aware of our own suffering most of the time, even to the point of obsession? What good does it do us?* Complaining and obsessing about our suffering is not what I mean by "connecting" to it. As long as I see my suffering as "mine," as unfair, as tragic, as something that should not have happened or should be removed, I am not really connecting to it. Quite the contrary, by thinking of the suffering as mine, as a mistake, and as something to be eliminated, I have reduced it to something manageable and at the same time distanced myself from it. To see my pain as "mine" and then to complain that it shouldn't be is to distract myself from it, to disconnect from it. I connect with my pain when I realize that it's not merely *my* pain—it is *the* pain, *the* human suffering, everyone's suffering.

This realization is what we are trying to avoid when we complain and wish that things were otherwise. Really connecting to our suffering seems so immense that we think it's unbearable. But we are quite wrong. To accept the immensity of our suffering is to find comfort in the heart of it. To connect this deeply with our own suffering is to open ourselves to the suffering of others and to be met in our own pain.

Once a woman came to the Buddha holding the corpse of her dead child, wailing in her anguish and pleading with the Buddha to bring the child back to life. The Buddha said that to do this he would need a rare ingredient: a mustard seed from the household of a family that had never known death. He sent the woman out to find such a mustard seed. But her desperate search yielded no such seed—only many stories of grief as great as and greater than her own. In the end these stories connected her deeply and truly to her own suffering, and so she was healed from her anguish.

It's easy to sympathize with the woman's feeling at the beginning of the story. The human desire to remove pain from our lives is strong. It is tough to connect to our pain so deeply that we see everyone's pain in it. We are so afraid of this that we do all that we can to avoid our pain, to run away from it if we can, to change or fix it somehow, or, if possible, to ignore it.

The most compelling form of pain avoidance is blaming. If you can occupy yourself enough with blaming your suffering on something or someone—even yourself—you don't have to notice the horrifying weight of your suffering. To feel that weight is to feel disempowered and weak. But when you blame, especially when you have some justification for blaming, you can replace the feeling of powerlessness with something much more energizing: anger and hatred. Now you are powerful, and you can do something to act out your power. Blaming brings a measure of satisfaction, even if it is yourself you are angry with, rail against, and sabotage, odd as that may seem. Knowing the culprit and going after him or her, you can safely avoid your sorrow and grief.

In my lifetime I have seen many instances of harbored anger and long-term grudges. Even when the parties involved have had sincere hearts and wanted very much to forgive each other, it was sometimes impossible for them to do so. In each and every case of forgiveness I have known, it occurred only when one of the parties, sometimes after years of denial, was finally able to fully connect to his or her own suffering and hurt. Then and only then could the heart soften toward the other person.

Forgiveness, then, isn't a special and unusual practice; it is the ongoing practice of accepting responsibility for your own difficulty. It is inner work. Reconciliation—reaching out to those who have wronged you or whom you have wronged—is another step. It comes out of our practice of forgiveness. Reconciliation requires us to understand the pain of the other person, without losing sight of our own pain, so that eventually we can express all the pain of the situation. In reconciliation we seek to make peace based on this recognition of the mutuality of pain. To reconcile is to balance appropriately one side with the other, until both sides of the scale come to rest.

We can't expect too much. The truth is that it is very difficult to communicate with someone when there is pain between you. There is a tremendous risk that the pain that caused the distance between you will so occlude communication that any effort to talk will lead to renewed pain. Sometimes reconciliation is impossible—at least for the moment. Maybe a lot of time has to go by before any effort to reconcile is even thinkable. Maybe it would be best to agree that nothing can be said without causing more trouble and to part company for a while with, if possible, a commitment to try again later.

Our personal lives are full of irreconcilable conflicts. Once two of my mother's sisters had a bitter argument over which of them was going to inherit a vase that my grandmother had owned. The vase was not particularly valuable or attractive, but the battle over it was intense and lasted for the rest of their lives—the sisters died without reconciling. Watching this conflict unfold over the course of many years, I eventually saw quite clearly that it was not about a vase at all (though this was not at all apparent to some other members of my family, who became fiercely partisan). The conflict was not even about my grandmother's death and the sisters' inability to digest and understand it. It was about a lifetime of unacknowledged conflict and suffering that hurt so badly that there would never be a way to overcome it, let alone recognize it for what it was. The sisters had hurt each other many times since childhood and had never been able to express that hurt until it erupted into open and permanent warfare over a vase. Such stories are not rare in families. And when they involve not only families but whole communities that have hurt each other over the generations, the scale of the tragedy becomes immense.

Many years ago our community suffered its most bitter crisis when our second abbot, Roshi Baker, resigned under fire. Many people left the community at that time, and the depth of hurt in those who left, as well as in those who remained, was immense. So many had felt betrayed—by Roshi Baker, by their friends in the community, by themselves for believing in what they now felt to be a foolish dream. The emotions were far too strong to deal with for many years. We simply had to wait them out. But after about fifteen years we were able to organize a retreat to try to open up and heal.

With Gary Friedman's help, we brought together about forty people who had been involved with the community in the days when all the trouble had happened, including Roshi Baker. We spent a weekend together practicing some meditation but mostly talking in the style of our reconciliation meetings. It was the most difficult and emotional weekend of my life. For hour after hour we listened to each other's stories, learning things about each other's inner lives we had never imagined. Although the meeting did not effect miraculous reconciliation, it did significantly change the hearts of many people. When you have a chance to hear another's sorrow, honestly told without blame or resistance, you see more clearly the large pattern of human hurting, and even if your pain remains so strong that you can't reconcile and make a new relationship, perhaps you can let go of some of the bitterness of the past.

In 1991 I led a Zen training period at our temple. The Gulf War had recently begun, and each day we would hear news of the killing. One of the women students had a son in the army who was stationed in the Persian Gulf. As is always the case in a war, the situation in the area was constantly changing, and the news was never complete or accurate. Every day this student feared that this would be the day her son went into combat, to kill or be killed. Her tension and fear became a major concern in all of our minds.

The theme of my talks was the Buddha's noble truth of suffering—accepting and understanding that all conditioned existence is of the nature of suffering, and that suffering is there-fore unavoidable and fundamental. When we accept and digest this fact, connecting to our own pain and through our pain to the suffering of others, we can find some peace, just as the woman looking for a mustard seed discovered. Although I en-couraged the efforts of our many students and supporters at the time who were protesting the Gulf War in an effort to stop it or slow it down, I also knew that humans have always been—and probably always will be—aggressive and violent, and that a true and deep vision of life requires us to know and accept this. Time and time again the woman whose son was in the army would cry out when I said this. She refused to hear it, to sit still for it. She could not even begin to accept the fact that her son might any day be put in the midst of such jeopardy.

And I knew that she was right. Suffering is inevitable and must be accepted. And yet, suffering is also unacceptable. The world is what it is; all we have to do is read the newspaper to see how full of pain the world is. Our anguish is only in-creased when our hope that the world will be different turns once again to disappointment: things haven't improved, civi-lization hasn't made us more humane. We despair that there will always be wars and famines, injustice and trouble. And yet, I also know that as human beings we must keep wanting the world and ourselves to be better than we are. So we have to hold both things in our minds and hearts at the same time: accepting what is, just as it is, and working to make it better some day. Accepting the war completely at the same time that we are trying to stop it.

Connection to our own suffering is connection to the full-ness of life. It brings us to a profound compassion for our-selves and others. The journey of maturity is long, sensitive, and essentially spiritual. It involves responding truly and faithfully to conditions, owning our own experience honestly without being limited by it, and developing the strength and stability to bear life's troubles and the self-acceptance necessary to be able truly to love others. None of this is possible if we ignore or avoid our suffering. Connecting to our pain is connecting to our life as bodhisattvas do—in identity and solidarity with the world, sharing its joys and its sorrows even though we know they are endless.

Six

MEDITATION

WHEN I WRITE ABOUT RELATIONSHIPS—ABOUT LISTENING, persistence, trust, connection, forgiveness, and all the other associated practices that build maturity—I seem to be assuming an abnormal human capacity for serious and deep attention. On the surface at least, it seems as if most of us are incapable of paying this much attention to our lives. We're all so harried, running around to take care of work, family, social engagements, entertainment, housekeeping, and so on. We are barely able to keep body and soul together, let alone be thoughtful and reflective about it all. Do any of us really have the time, let alone the psychic space, to nurture ourselves sufficiently so that we can grow and mellow into the people we most fundamentally are?

I see the problem, but I am not discouraged by it. I am sure that everyone has the capacity to develop profound attentiveness—and moreover, I know that everyone longs and needs to develop it. Our lives cry out for attentiveness, our hearts yearn for it.

Developing attentiveness doesn't take extra time. It's not an additional item on our already full "to do" lists. Rather, attentiveness is the spirit, the style, the attitude, and the skill with we approach those lists. In fact, attentiveness saves time. It eliminates automatically the many extra items that are on our lists because we lacked attentiveness in the first place. With attentiveness we don't complicate things so much—we don't mindlessly create messes that require more activity to sort out. With attentiveness we naturally review and reorient priorities, and our lists slowly change character, becoming simpler. Although it makes no sense to say that we are too busy to be attentive, it is true that attentiveness must be cultivated. The best way to cultivate attention is through meditation practice.

Soon after Rashid's impassioned outburst about his parents' separation, the boys and I decided to practice meditation in our meetings. We experimented with different forms of meditation and eventually found the practices that became our own. We began our meetings with an offering practice, traditional in Buddhism, but almost universal in spiritual traditions: mindfully making symbolic gestures of gratitude for our lives, accompanied by words or silent intentions of aspiration for spiritual growth. We offered incense before the Buddha image on an altar that also included a lit candle and fresh flowers.

Many kinds of altars are possible. Your altar could be built around a picture of Jesus or Mary, a copy of the Koran or the Bible, a picture of a mountain or a sunset, or simply a stone or a pinecone. And the offering can be anything—an apple, clear water, a treat. It is not the details that are important but the feeling the altar represents or evokes of peacefulness, reverence, gratitude, and spiritual aspiration.

The boys and I made our offerings in silence. Carefully,

each boy would take his turn placing the lit incense in the pot. Sometimes we spoke words of dedication as we made the offering gesture ("With this incense offering may we find the way to a true maturity that benefits all humankind"), and sometimes we were silent with our own feelings.

After the incense offering, we moved silently into a meditation practice in which we chanted the Japanese syllables *namu dai bo sa* ("I identify with the great bodhisattva"). I had learned this chant from the late Maurine Stuart, one of my Zen teachers, and whenever I chant it I think of her belting it out in her strong, clear alto voice. I taught it to the boys, and they liked it, so we chanted it at each meeting, rhythmically over and over to the accompaniment of a small Korean drum. At first the chanting would be a little ragged, and we were self-conscious about it, but as we persisted our voices gradually began to blend, until we made one sound together that seemed to go deep inside. After the chanting, the silence in the room was strong. We sat in its midst for a few minutes, paying attention to breathing in and out. We chanted a Japanese Zen phrase, but other phrases can be used. The practice of chanting or singing, like offering, is also common to most spiritual traditions.

Our third practice was the bell meditation. I had a good, small Japanese meditation bell with a clear, reverberating sound. One of us would strike the bell (we took turns), and then we sat quietly listening as closely as we could to the rising, swelling, and disappearing of the sound, to the silence that succeeded the sound, to the ambient noises that then filled the silence, and then to the sound coming back when the bell was struck another time. The boys' imaginations were captured by the notion of trying to find that elusive place where the sound of the bell disappears into silence. We struck the bell six times, with lots of space in between each striking. After the sixth time, we again sat quietly in meditation for a few minutes, breathing and paying attention to the feeling of our bodies. This three-practice routine at the beginning and end of each meeting became our custom and made a difference in the kind of conversation we were able to have together.

When I first began meditation practice more than thirty years ago, most people thought of it as something inherently Asian and therefore unnatural for Westerners to do. D. T. Suzuki, the early Zen pioneer in America whose books I had read as a college student, felt that Western people would never be able to do classical meditation practice and that they would come to spiritual insight through books, reflection, and conversation with adepts like himself. But Suzuki was quite wrong. Meditation practice isn't Asian—it isn't even Buddhist or Hindu. It is human. Anyone can do it, and today, in the West, millions do.

Meditation practice does calm us down—and this is important—but it is much more than a tranquilizing technique. Meditation practice is a powerful way of getting deeply in touch with your life at its most essential level. As you become more in touch with your life at this level, you naturally become more attentive, awake, and attuned to your thoughts, emotions, and inner currents. Meditation practice is a spiritual process that unfolds with your life. It requires no doctrine or belief system, and it can be adapted to many purposes and systems of thought. In its broadest sense, meditation practice is an approach to life that promotes self-awareness, self-kindness, and self-forgiveness and brings us the clarity to see what we need to do in our lives and the forbearance to stay the course. Meditation practice fosters the calmness and balance that enable us to be honest with our emotions and needs without being limited and trapped by them. Meditation practice makes it more possible for us to act out of our deepest, calmest, most accurate selves.

In short, meditation practice helps us to firmly set the cornerstone of the most important relationship of our lives: our relationship with our self. As this relationship develops, our meditation opens up to include others; and as our relationships soften and deepen, loving kindness and openness become more natural to us. Meditation practice nourishes our maturity.

While I am convinced of the efficacy of meditation practice and know that ordinary people can do it in the context of ordinary lives, I don't want to underestimate the difficulty. Although anyone can meditate for ten or twenty minutes once in a while, the real fruits of meditation practice require some commitment, some discipline, and some courage.

In Asia over the generations meditation practice has been the province of monastics. By and large meditation has not been practiced by ordinary people, who have imagined that it requires a level of truth-seeking and determination far beyond what they could muster. "Maybe next lifetime," the faithful would typically say. In the West, too, contemplative life has been largely monastic, requiring total commitment and great self-sacrifice. Zen, too, is essentially monastic, and has a reputation as a fairly rigorous discipline. Certainly the stories of the tough old Chinese Zen masters, who sat without moving for days at a time and shouted at their students when they weren't whacking them with sticks, make Zen meditation practice seem pretty daunting.

It is true that meditation practice is not for the fainthearted. I have always felt, however, that a life inspired by disciplined meditation practice (or some other form of spiritual endeavor) is easy compared to the alternative: the rigors and travails of ordinary life. Especially these days, with traffic snarls, media blizzards, the dizzying upturns and downturns of the economy, and the consequent twin epidemics of busyness and stress, just getting through an average day takes a great deal of fortitude. It seems to me that no form of austere monasticism is more difficult than this. During all the years I spent living in Zen temples, rising early in the morning to meditate and chant, and then working all day, I always felt that what I was doing was quite easy compared to nonmonastic life.

But ordinary life has always been difficult and rigorous. There's an old story about the "bird's nest Roshi," a Zen teacher of the T'ang dynasty who practiced meditation in a bird's nest up in a tree branch. The branch was high up in a tall tree, which was exactly the point: the Roshi sat up there to force himself to stay awake and alert. If he dozed off, he'd surely fall and kill himself. The Chinese poet Po Chu I, who was a government official, came to visit and called up to the Roshi: "Why do you meditate up there? It's so dangerous." The bird's nest Roshi replied: "It may look dangerous to you, but to me, being down there is far more dangerous."

In its simplest and most basic forms, meditation is stopping your complicated activity for a while and taking time to focus your mind steadily on one thing. The more useless that thing is the better, because if it is something useful—a task or a problem, for instance—your mind is likely to become too interested in it. When the mind is too interested in something, it wants to do something with it, and desire activates the mind, causing it to search for solutions, run through possibilities, project into the future, review the past. With meditation you want the mind to be bright and alert but calm, so the meditation object should be something definite enough to hold on to but not so thrilling that you get excited about it. It's good to use something like the breath, or the posture, or simple physical sensations.

After trying and failing to anchor the mind on one or more of these things, you might well get a bit frustrated. And frustration, as we've seen, is very useful because it promotes the practice of persistence. The more you practice meditation, the more you appreciate that it is less a matter of actual meditation on the object than it is a matter of persisting in coming back over and over again to the object when you have lost track of it. As any meditator knows, the mind's tendency to distraction is prodigious. The mind won't stay put! So you gently persist in your efforts to train the mind as you would persist in training a small child or an animal—with patience and much repetition.

Trying to focus the mind on an object but being unable to do it for very long, despite all our efforts, is a humbling experience, and that in itself is something quite useful. With practice over time, however, it does become easier to settle the mind, slow it down, calm it, sharpen it, stabilize it. With this stabilization come many physical changes. The heartbeat, breath, and brain activity all slow down. The whole body enters a state of restfulness and calm. It is the production of these physical changes that makes meditation so useful for our health and well-being.

When the body is calm and the breath comes strongly into focus, thoughts are less compelling, and less deceptive. We feel emotions strongly, but they do not have as much power over us as they usually do. Our emotions are less seductive, less obsessive. We see and experience what's going on inside us with much more accuracy.

It is this capacity to clearly see our attitudes, thoughts, and emotions that makes meditation practice so important for the development of maturity. Once the mind slows down and is relieved of its various jobs and projects, it becomes simply present, alert but not anxious, and things get interesting. We begin to notice and experience things we never noticed or experienced before. We see the subtle patterns of thought and feeling that ceaselessly arise and pass away in our minds—patterns, we realize, that were probably present all along but that we never noticed before. For most of us it is initially quite a shock to see close-up how often we are petty, greedy, jealous, lazy, stupid, dull, or confused, how often we repeat ourselves, daydream, gripe, or speculate wildly, how radically dissatisfied and restless we are so much of the time.

As you continue to meditate and to notice these patterns you may well begin wondering whether it was a good idea to begin meditation practice in the first place. Before meditation practice none of the patterns you're noticing were a problem, because you didn't notice them. Or perhaps the meditation practice is producing more of these troubling mental states than you would otherwise have been experiencing. Maybe you were better off before. Maybe meditation practice is making your life worse! I have heard such doubts expressed by many students over the years, but they are always expressed with a certain bemused humor, as if the meditation practice they have done has given them a sense of well-being that is somewhat in advance of their capacity to think about it.

Of course, meditation practice doesn't make your life worse, it makes it better. But it makes your life better the way most things that are lasting and important do—by a long and circuitous route. Meditation practice improves your life by showing you, first of all, with some difficult clarity, the mess you are in. Indeed, you see that you've been in this mess all along but never noticed it before. Most of us do not like to think we are in a mess. We are well conditioned to put the best face on things, to be cheerful, to look the other way if something unpleasant comes up. It is ordinary common sense: to hope for the best and act as if everything were for the best. Often we behave like those three monkeys who cover up eyes, ears, and mouth to see no evil, hear no evil, and speak no evil. Who wants to look at unpleasantness, to dredge it up, to dwell on it? And besides, none of us wants to see ourselves as someone with problems, someone who needs help, someone who is not doing terribly well. So we don't see our true condition, and we don't particularly want to see it. Even if once in a while we do get a glimpse of how things really are with us, we dismiss it as an aberration, just a bad day or week, and try our best to distract ourselves, to stay busy, to go on to other things.

If you were someone who doesn't like to see difficulty and strongly prefers to deny or ignore it, you probably wouldn't be interested in meditation in the first place. Meditation would seem threatening at worst and boring at best. Why waste time sitting around doing nothing when there's so much to do, especially if the sitting around doing nothing is going to make you brood on how much you are failing as a human being! Where's the advantage in that?

Anyone who's interested in meditation in the first place probably already senses that we are all in a mess, the human mess, and that we have no choice but to clean it up. People who are ill—with heart conditions or cancer or stress-related illnesses or simply greater-than-average unhappiness—or people who have been deeply affected by profound experiences of death or loss are strongly motivated meditators. They have been forced to recognize the inescapable truth that life isn't easy and smooth, that it inevitably brings problems, that going along with business as usual as if none of this were so is simply not sustainable. Such people have realized that life is always in crisis, not only for them but for everyone. Meditation practice helps us to face this crisis as it really is and nourishes our process for working on it.

When you begin to admit that there is a mess, and then to view the mess with calmness and accuracy, the mess becomes less threatening. It becomes interesting. You appreciate the beauty of its shape and pattern. You gradually come to see that the mess isn't so bad really. It's just that you have been adding a mess on top of your mess, making matters worse in your life by not paying attention to the way you have been living or to your thoughts and emotions. Without knowing what you were doing, you set in motion habits of mind that emphasize trouble and make it worse and that deemphasize—or sometimes miss altogether—wholesome and helpful states of mind and heart. Sitting on your meditation chair or cushion, you begin to see more and more clearly how this is so. And once you begin to see more clearly, you begin to change, even without trying to. Naturally, without any special effort, the awareness that meditation promotes inspires you to gradually let go of your strong habit of making matters worse. Seeing your life more clearly helps you to do what comes naturally to all of us: encourage what makes us happy and let go of what makes us suffer.

As you continue meditating, other fundamental insights begin to come into view. You see that your sense of self is not as fixed as you once believed it was. Rather than being some essence of "me-ness" that is somehow inside you or enclosing you, you see that your sense of self is a fluid series of experiences, impressions, feelings, attitudes. You begin to see how much of a burden it has been to try to shore all of that up into a concept of "me" that you have spent your life defending, justifying, building up, and sometimes self-destructively and painfully tearing down without realizing you were doing this. You can feel how much pain this burden of "me" has caused you, in small ways every day and in large and tragic ways through the major crises of your life. You realize that much of that wasn't necessary, that your "me" never needed defending in the first place. Within the wider space of your meditation practice your "me" seems to come and go with flexibility and ease. Even when your concept of self is painful, you see how the very painfulness has within it a path toward release, for you come to know that your pain has come not from the "me" itself, but from your clutching it so tightly, and that once you relax your hold you find peace. And sometimes, when your mind is very quiet, the sense of self isn't even there at all. There's only the feeling of being, without any particular boundaries or issues.

As you sit in your meditation place trying to quiet your mind, day after day, year after year, you realize that the fundamental basis of your life is not, as you had always imagined, "me." The primary fact of your life, and of all life, is that everything changes ceaselessly. Sounds, images, sensations, thoughts, feelings, memories—all come and go. The body isn't a thing, it's a process. Your breathing circulates endlessly. Your heart beats. Sitting there, your body doesn't feel like an object, it feels like a living world, always in flux, always new. Moments waft by like smoke. Life is fleeting, ever-changing, tragic, joyous, precious, precise. When we appreciate all of this as the fruit of our meditation practice, we no longer hang on so hard to the mundane "me" aspect of things. We don't get so tangled up in our own lives. We don't create so much trouble for ourselves or others.

Meditation practice shows us the power of presence in our lives. We are alive only in the present: the past is memory and the future is speculation. But this present has no boundary. You feel this on your meditation cushion, where with each silent moment of full awareness, past, present, and future meet. Every present moment carries with it the past's conditioning and the future's seed, so every present moment freshly offers the possibility of redemption from what has been and the healing into what will be. Meditation practice doesn't cause this to be so. It simply is so and has always been so. Meditation practice only helps us to appreciate it.

A Zen koan makes this point in a few words. Damei asks Mazu, "What is Buddha?" Mazu answers, "This very mind is Buddha!"

To simply be present with our lives at the depth that meditation practice can take us to is a profound accomplishment. To inhabit our lives in this way is to meet and become the Buddha, to be touched by and to touch the divine. Cutting through our entanglements without denying them, we reach the ultimate, not by an act of transcendence, but simply by living with full awareness.

How exactly do we practice meditation? First, remember that the essence of meditation practice is focusing the mind calmly. This is the fundamental thing. You don't have to twist your legs up into a pretzel and sit rigidly upright. Still, the yogic posture called the full lotus, in which you fold your right leg on top of your left thigh and your left leg on top of your right thigh so that you are sitting with your feet in your lap, was not a creation of masochists or fools. In fact, this posture (or one of its many variations) is very stable and helps you keep your back fairly straight, which is important. But you don't need to assume the lotus posture in order to meditate.

For basic mediation, take a seat, either on a meditation cushion or on a chair. This could be a straight-backed chair or a comfortable chair or couch. You want to be comfortable, but remember, though meditation may be deeply relaxing, the point is not relaxation in and of itself. The purpose of meditation is seeing our lives as they really are. This accurate seeing takes alertness and awareness, so you do not want to lounge or recline (unless, because of an illness or injury, there is no other way). I usually recommend that meditators sit up straight without leaning on the back of the chair or couch, so that the back supports itself. This is possible for most people; if you have a weak back or a back injury, you might have to use the back of the chair for support.

Sit on the chair, couch, or cushion squarely and evenly. Check out your rear end to make sure that the sitting bones are firmly on the seat. (If you are on a cushion, you'll want to sit at the edge of it, not squarely in the center, so that the cushion is just a wedge supporting you.) Stretch the back top of your head up toward the ceiling. Tuck your chin in. Lift up your chest and pull your shoulders back a little, but don't tense them. Let your shoulders drop. Rotate your pelvis forward and arch the lower back slightly inward: this movement will naturally lift up the upper body, stretching the spine so that you are sitting up straight, without constriction. Posture is important and something to work with; though sitting up straight may feel unnatural at first, it will feel more natural as you continue to practice. Fold your hands in your lap or place them on your knees palms down or up, whichever way is comfortable for you.

Once you have settled into your posture, bring your attention to your lower belly and see how it moves with your breathing. Without manipulating your breathing in any way, just pay attention to the rising and falling of the belly that happens with each breath in and out. Keep your eyes half open, gazing out in front of you. If you can sit facing a blank wall, which is preferable, lower your gaze and look at the wall, without focusing your eyes too much. Keep your mouth closed, but don't clench your jaw. Let your tongue rest on the roof of your mouth and touch the back of your front teeth, as it naturally will. Wear comfortable, nonconstricting clothing so that the abdomen area can be as open as possible. Count exhales silently, beginning with one and going up to ten. If you lose count, go back to one without blame or worry. This is not a contest. If you get to ten, go back to one again.

After a while, you can leave off counting if you like and just sit peacefully but alertly following each breath, in and out, in the lower belly. If you feel sensations in the body (like ache, warmth, or release), or if you notice thoughts or emotions arising (which you no doubt will), treat them all the same way: pay attention, but do not get too interested or complain too much. As soon as you notice your preoccupation with a thought, emotion, or physical sensation, use that very thing as a cue to come back to awareness of posture and breathing in the belly.

If you need to move your posture or take a rest, allow yourself to explore your discomfort for a few breaths before you relieve it. This can be extremely instructive and helpful. If you find you are getting drowsy because you are too relaxed, try to sit up a little straighter or open your eyes wider to try to rouse yourself. Pay attention to whatever light there is in the room. (You don't want to meditate in a room that's too dark, but a glaring light is no good either.) If you are really sleepy, then stand up and continue the practice in the same way standing with your hands at your sides. I usually recommend that people meditate for twenty to thirty minutes a day—long enough to begin to settle the mind, but not so long that it gets tiresome or too tough. It is good to sit regularly, with a firm commitment. Meditating now and then when you feel like it, or when you feel you need to, is not as good. Remember the practice of persistence!

This basic technique of Zen meditation is done in many other schools of Buddhism as well. Catholic monks and laypeople practice it in monasteries and retreat centers, rabbis and their congregants practice it in synagogues, people in clinics, jails, workplaces, and in homes practice it. There is nothing particularly Zen about this technique. I think of it as basic human meditation.

Note the sheer physicality of the practice. In Japanese it is called, literally, "just sitting"—in other words, simply being present with the fact of being alive, breathing, in the body. It is such a simple thing, and yet so profound, to appreciate directly that we are living, breathing bodies. Mostly we take this for granted and occupy ourselves with what seem like more significant concerns. But in fact, there is nothing more significant than being our bodies. Meditation practice is a physical practice. In the West many centuries of philosophical thought have produced a deeply embedded belief that the mind and body are split off from each other. We assume that our essential selves reside in our minds, in our personalities, in our wills, or in our intellects. The Western mind-body split leads us to assume that spiritual practice, of all things, is not physically determined.

One of the most important of all early Buddhist texts, the Mindfulness Sutra, says that awareness practice is the only way to spiritual opening, and that awareness practice begins with awareness of the body in all its dimensions, from the simplest (awareness of standing or sitting, awareness of breathing) to the most complex (awareness of the composite and impermanent nature of the body). The sutra goes on to show that the practice of awareness of the body is a foundation for the practices of awareness of the mind and its states, which are in turn supports for awareness of the deepest spiritual truths. The path begins with, and is grounded in, awareness of the body.

Most of us, however, have very confused relationships with our own bodies. We objectify them and see them as a presentation of ourselves—one that most of us are ashamed of, or at the very least are alienated from. We look in the mirror and think that what we see there is us. We judge the body critically and are forever imagining ways it could be improved. But in fact what we see in the mirror is not the body. The real body, as meditation practice shows us, is not an image. It is a set of experiences and sensations, a complex of inside and outside, a vast and nearly unknown plethora of activity. The heartbeat, the workings of the organs, the breath—these activities are also the body. Alternating sensations of cold and heat, hardness and softness, heaviness and lightness; thoughts associated with aches or pains; emotions that tense or relax the limbs or organs; wishes, dreams, and fleshly desires—all of this, too, is the body. Who can encompass the body's dimension? Who can explain its functioning?

We don't know the body, and we don't know the mind either. We cover our thoughts with "shoulds" and "oughts," or with dullness and distraction. Most of the time we really don't know how we feel, what we love, what we fear, what we desire. We aren't even all that clear about what we see, hear, taste, touch, and smell. Meditation practice serves little by little to introduce us to the complicated and not easily categorized person we call our self. Little by little, if we persist in our practice, we find ourselves establishing a warm and realistic relationship with this person, and that will be the basis for forging warm and realistic relationships with others and with the world.

In one of his many commentaries on Hasidic teachings, Martin Buber cites one old rabbi who taught that everything depends on oneself. "When a man has made peace within himself," Buber writes, "he will be able to make peace in the whole world." Buber speaks of the necessity of our "decision" to "straighten ourselves out" so that we can straighten out the world. We do this, he says, by aligning ourselves with ourselves, so that our deep inner conflicts can be healed.

Buber is telling us that so long as our relationship with ourselves is awry, the whole world remains awry. How can this be so? How can making friends with ourselves affect the world? Am I so self-centered as to think that I am the center of the universe, and that somehow when I am happy the whole world is going to stand up and rejoice? Here we come to the deepest aspect of meditation practice. The paradox is that when we enter into true friendship with ourselves, we see that we are not atomized individuals separate from and opposed to the world. Being aware of the body and the mind as acutely, alertly, and peacefully as possible, I become aware of that which is larger than myself, which holds me in its embrace, and which is what I truly am, was before I was born, and will be after I leave this life.

This is what I have appreciated in my meditation practice over the years. It is why as time goes on I have been seeing less and less difference between the silent meditation I practice and the many other forms of spiritual practice that exist in this world. To me sitting in open silence is a prayer. It is the prayer of the body, the wordless prayer of the world. And when I do engage in formal prayer, as I sometimes do, it feels the same to me. Sitting in open silence is also a ritual: it is the ritual of the body, of the breath.

Yet meditation practice isn't something special. Fundamentally, it is just life, life in its fullness and depth. Can we experience life at this level without the aid of technique, without prayer, without meditation practice, without ritual? We can, and sometimes we do. But meditation practice helps to remind us of what our life really is. It inspires us and makes it more possible for us to develop the many personal qualities we need to go on with the real work of growing up.

About a month after Rashid's outburst, Sam's elderly grandfather fell ill, and Sam and his parents traveled back east to see him. While they were there, his grandfather died. After Sam returned to, he was eager to talk about it. He said, "When Grandpa died a space opened up in the room. You could feel the space glowing around him just when he was nearest to dying. Then after he died, it glowed even stronger until the nurse took him out.

"Afterward I felt very quiet. I went outside into the woods past the hospital grounds. The leaves were beginning to turn. I saw one leaf twist off its stem and float down. Then it blew up again. When it finally landed it disappeared into all the other leaves. My father said this is like meditation practice. The big space, I mean. I think we should do meditation practice at our meetings."

That was how our mentoring group began to meditate.

Seven

V O W I N G

WHEN I HAD ORIGINALLY THOUGHT ABOUT WHAT IT MIGHT be like to engage in a discussion about life with four teenage boys, I was skeptical. How would I keep a conversation going? I tried my best to come up with techniques and tricks and ways of presenting things that would keep their interest alive. But I had not figured on the eruption of dramatic life events into the process. Now it seemed obvious that such things were bound to happen.

The death of Sam's grandfather and his subsequent grieving and questioning; the separation of Rashid's parents and his forgiving them through confronting his own pain—these happenings were like stones dropped into the pond of our conversation: they made initial splashes, and then many ripples radiating outward. As the weeks went by we found ourselves talking, quite personally and passionately, about many things—suffering, parents, romantic relationships, death, spirituality.

Whenever you go on with something long enough—whether it is a group like ours, a relationship, a task, or a discipline—inevitably things happen that will shape events beyond anyone's ability to foresee them. If you are open to what occurs and welcome it even if it is something difficult, as Sam and Rashid did, things usually turn out all right. Whatever happens can be grist for the mill.

The group was becoming lively and engaging. I looked forward to the meetings, and I think the boys did, too. The meditation practices we were now doing only increased the range and depth of what we talked about. But not all the boys were equally engaged. Of the four of them, Tony still remained somewhat aloof. Although there were moments when he seemed as enthusiastic as the others, his initial sullenness hadn't changed all that much. So I was quite surprised when one day he announced to us all that he intended to take Zen lay vows, committing himself in a formal ceremony to the Zen ethical precepts.

The other boys didn't know what to make of this, and Tony's explanations about his decision were abstract and hard to follow. When I had a chance to talk to him about it later, he was reluctant to speak at first. But finally he said that what was bothering him, and had been bothering him for a long time, was that he was bored. He wasn't interested in school, he wasn't interested in social life, he wasn't interested in sports, he wasn't interested in anything.

"That was okay before," he said, "when I was ten or twelve. Then I could just stay in my room and play or watch TV. But now I need something to go on, some kind of an idea." And since he could find no such idea anywhere in the world he saw around him, he decided that he would make his own idea, out of a vow. Although he didn't have much sense of what the Zen vows actually meant, he had seen the impressive ceremony performed when he was a child and was quite sure that this was the answer to his problems. I felt as though he needed to think about this step further, so from then on vowing and ethical conduct became new topics for our group discussions. At last Tony's interest was piqued.

I BELIEVE WE ARE BORN WITH VOWS. AS CHILDREN WE KNOW this. We feel instinctively the power of our vowing, of the deep intentions inside us we know we must live out somehow. This vowing power is what makes childhood so rich and mysterious. Childhood's world is full of magic and story, and each event is a contributory detail in the tale of our inner journey toward the fulfillment of our heart's desire. All children hold vows to learn, to grow, to create, to love, to experience, to plunge forward into the endless and unknowable future. Although as they grow older children forget these vows—and the many other vows they find inside themselves—they do not forget entirely. Vowing remains a latent force in our lives, no matter how hidden it may seem.

Earlier I spoke about my childhood vow not to grow up, a vow that conditioned my life in many ways. I am sure that following it and allowing it to transform into something clearer and deeper was responsible for my decision to choose the spiritual life. But I had other vows as well. I can remember sitting in a Sunday school classroom one day and hearing the sad and inspiring stories of the Jewish martyrs, stories that frightened and impressed me. I felt myself sitting in my seat at that moment as though it were an eternal moment, and I thought, *I will be like that, too: I will never give up what I am, never give up what I know to be so, because someone tries to force me to.* I felt that because of what people before me had endured in being true to their deepest identities and commitments, I, too, would endure and remain steadfast, in their honor and in their name. As a Jewish child listening to a Jewish tale, I felt a vow come upon me to hold fast to being a Jew no matter what, a vow I have always kept in my heart, despite the fact that I have practiced Buddhism for so long.

I am sure that all of us, if we remember our lives deeply enough, could uncover vows that spontaneously arose in our earlier days. Those vows reenter our conscious minds and willing hearts when we are ready for them, when we really need them, when our sufferings, our disappointments, our life's trials, bring them to the surface. Sometimes it's our joys that do this: our love and devotion to another person causes us to remember our vow to keep a tender heart, to remain open to love. Awakened anew to these old vows, we make a new, adult vow to share our life with another person. And sometimes, without any particular provocation but simply through our living, our deepest vows float back into our consciousness: the vow to be a good person, to live as truthfully, deeply, and beautifully as the heroes who strode through the stories we heard when we were young.

Earlier I described connection to our own pain as the beginning, the seed, of our maturity. We can't attain true maturity until we see life as it really is, with all its difficult realities and our own limitations. Meditation practice is the nutrient that this seed of maturity needs for its sustained development. Meditation—the practice of fundamental awareness—promotes engagement with our whole life, inner as well as outer, and enables us to grow into the human beings we were made to be. Vowing is the next step. A seed that has been planted and nurtured must be watered so that its roots will go deep. By our vow we deepen and anchor our lives.

When you vow, you get in touch with and give yourself completely to what matters most: the experience of receiving an inner calling and answering that calling with your whole life. The vowing life begins intimately and personally but expands outward, bringing the passion of the personal, through discipline and commitment over time, to deeper and wider realms.

There are many ways to live a life of vowing. I have known people who live their vow through art or work or service; others do it simply by remaining for a long time in a particular place that they have come to know well and to love. Perhaps most movingly, I have also known people for whom the need to overcome great suffering—personal tragedies like abuse or loss, social forces like sexism, racism, or homophobia, a physical or mental illness, the long tragic course of an addiction— has been a vital and courageous path of vowing.

Vows are energies. Vows are aspirations. They are larger than life. Endless sources of inspiration, vows differ from goals, which are limited in scope. Goals can be met. Vows can be practiced but never exactly completed, for they are essentially unfulfillable, and it is their very inexhaustibility that propels us forward, opens us up, shapes our desires and actions.

One of my Zen teachers, Roshi Bernie Glassman, once vowed to end homelessness, an absolutely preposterous idea. How could one person, even with many helpers, end homelessness? And this was a religious person—a meditation master—without connections, resources, or skills suited to the task. And yet, through the power of his vow, Bernie established the Greyston Foundation, a network of social service agencies in Yonkers, New York, that house the homeless, educate their children, and offer them jobs, job training, counseling, and other services. I visited Greyston recently and was astonished to see how much had come from one person's devotion to an impossible vow. Did Bernie actually end homelessness? No, not at all. Are there fewer homeless people today than there were when Bernie began to practice his vow? I don't know and neither does he. But it makes no difference. Bernie goes on practicing his vow.

If vows are unfulfillable, why undertake them? Why frustrate ourselves trying to do the impossible? Because this is how we are: making vows is what we seem to need to do to find a deep sense of satisfaction. Unlike all other beings, who live entirely in the world of actuality, human beings live in two worlds: one that is, and one that isn't. We can imagine and long for a world that doesn't exist and might never exist. A world without homelessness or war. A world with more love than hate. Such a world can be as real to us as the earth we walk on. We can contemplate it and yearn for it even if it is utterly impossible. Vows are the vehicles for that contemplation. They transform contemplation from mere abstract musing into the driving force of a lifetime.

The power and immensity of vowing began to dawn on the boys and me as our discussions continued. The idea surfaced that we might all want to take vows—not just Tony—as part of the process of our group. This idea terrified James, and he said so. It was too heavy, too serious, too stark a possibility. But James couldn't simply say no. A very competitive boy, he felt challenged by Tony's unwavering decision to take the Zen vows. If Tony was determined to do this, James thought, maybe he should be doing it, too. Why would he not do it? Because he was afraid? Because he was too immature?

Although at this point the other boys didn't see themselves taking vows, the conversation challenged them, too. It made them realize that they were getting older and coming to the time in their lives when they would be faced with consequential choices—inescapable and decisive choices that would shape them forever. Only Tony seemed undaunted by this prospect. He seemed to thrive on the idea of making vows and binding choices. It was as if he wanted to plunge as quickly as possibly into the problems of adult life, if only to present himself with a challenge that would be exciting and dangerous. His resolve to take Zen vows remained firm. Something about vowing appealed to that part of him that had played endless superhero games when he was a child.

Indeed, vowing is risky. Even as benign and ordinary a vow as the wedding vow commits us to "plight our troth" (put our personal truth at risk) in our commitment to our marriage partner and to "love, honor, and cherish" him or her, regardless of what the future brings. Insofar as vowing sets us on a course of action beyond what we may desire or can control, it is always challenging. The dictates of our vow may well run counter to our wishes and apparent self-interest. Being true to our vow may force us into difficult decisions or heroic actions. Vowing opens us up to self-transcendence and destiny. It is a path that could easily involve hardship.

One of the most drastic and problematic stories of vowing in all of world literature is the story of Abraham and Isaac, one of the tales on the Bible stories record I listened to as a child. As many times as I heard it, it never failed to raise the hair on my neck. The faithful Abraham, God's devoted servant, prays for many years for a child with his wife, Sarah, until finally (when they are both in their nineties!) God preposterously proposes to give them a son. Husband and wife both laugh at the idea, but the son is born and grows up healthy. Of course they adore him. Then God commands the sacrifice of that very son, "Isaac, your favored son, the one you love." Abraham and Isaac slowly and silently walk together up to the top of Mount Moriah, the mountain of sacrifice. The servant boy has been told to stay behind. Isaac carries firewood. Abraham carries a knife and the fire to be used for the offering pyre. Isaac asks, "But what shall we sacrifice?" "Don't worry, son," Abraham replies. "God will provide."

Any child of any parent—if he or she has any imagination at all—is going to be affected by this story. Fear is probably the first and foremost reaction. Betrayal. Confusion. Shock. The irrationality and cruelty of God's request. The monstrosity of it. And the obedience of Abraham, the blind trust he has in his God. Although there are passages in the Bible where characters protest mightily against God's commands (as Abraham himself does when God becomes angry and wants to destroy the cities of Sodom and Gommorah), here there is no such reaction. Abraham goes along silently with God's order. He rises early in the morning to carry it out, diligently and methodically. Nothing is said about how he feels or what goes through his mind as he walks up that steep trail side by side with his unsuspecting son.

Probably no story in world literature has been discussed and commented on as frequently as this one. My own feeling for it has changed over the years. When I was young, I considered the story a scandal and an affront. How ridiculous of God to craft such a test, how sinister, how bullying. And Abraham—where is his nerve? Why doesn't he scream and curse? Job does. Why doesn't he simply refuse? Jonah does. What's the worst that can happen to Abraham? If God kills him, so what? Who wouldn't choose to die in place of his own son, to die rather than carry out such a hideous request? Is Abraham merely a coward? Is his fear stronger than his love? Does his fanatical blind faith cause him to lose sight of all human decency, not to say nobility? Or is he simply too stupid to conceive of the idea of disobedience?

Later I came to feel that it is neither fear nor stupidity nor fanaticism that motivates Abraham, but devotion. Not devotion to a person, to a sense of duty, or even to an idea or creed, and not to his own integrity. Devotion rather to the vow he made to God, who I now knew not as the stern and bullying father represented by the booming male voice on my childhood record, but as the vast all-inclusiveness, the universally connected immensity of reality we all share. Not everyone may be comfortable with this or any other idea of God, but most people can feel that there is a powerful mystery at the heart of being. It is this mystery that is the ultimate ground of vowing. And this is why vowing seems so frightening.

Most of us don't think much about this immense and mysterious aspect of our lives. Most of the time we are too busy or engaged to think about it. This mystery seems quite irrelevant to our many problems and concerns. What does it have to do with our work, our friendships and family, our effort to simply get through the day? And yet, where would we be without it, this immense and ineffable spaciousness out of which we have come and to which we return?

Abraham knows this mystery and takes it personally. Somehow it is as palpable to him as dirt, as real as his own heartbeat. Impassioned by it, he trudges up that trail. The sacrifice he is prepared to offer makes no sense in any ordinary terms. Sacrificing his son is simply wrong, even insane. But Abraham's vow to remain true to the mystery, dangerous as it might be, takes him beyond himself. He lives not by his own lights but by the vow. He trusts that what is right and good for his life will transpire, even though he cannot see it. He gives up control, but he does not give up choice: he chooses trust.

In the end Abraham is not required to sacrifice Isaac. His faithfulness to his vow proves to be stronger than the harshness of God's test. Perhaps Abraham knows all along that this will be the outcome. Perhaps he walks up that mountain with serenity and confidence, knowing that as long as he holds to his ultimate vow of trusting the mystery, no evil can possibly occur, that God must be, in the end, good. Or perhaps, being human and therefore subject always to doubt, he still feels a powerful fear despite his perfect faith.

Vowing is never an easy path, but life isn't easy. We have all been brought up to deny this. Like the Buddha's parents, our own parents tried to protect us from the harsh side of life so that we would grow up with a sense that the world is fair, pleasant, and manageable. Maybe they wished this were really so and hoped that they could actually make it so for us. But they did not succeed, for life's troubles cannot be eliminated. Only something as thoroughgoing as vowing is strong enough to overcome our deep underlying disappointment and dismay about how life really is.

I've used as a theme for this book the Buddhist notion of the bodhisattva, the enthusiastic "enlightening" being who is dedicated to the work of maturing others. In their dedication to the ultimate welfare of all beings, bodhisattvas make heroic efforts over many lifetimes. They also make heroic vows. In Zen temples all over the world the four great bodhisattva vows are chanted daily: to benefit an infinite number of beings; to clarify an infinite amount of delusion; to do an infinite amount of good; and to completely become this infinite vow.

Like Roshi Bernie's vow to end homelessness, the four great bodhisattva vows are impossible to fulfill. One can benefit many beings, but not an infinite number; one can clarify a certain amount of delusion, perhaps even a great deal, but not an infinite amount. The four great bodhisattva vows are impossibly idealistic on purpose, for such idealism is a necessity for human beings, who are creatures capable of imagining infinite worlds that might be and are not. Because of the inexhaustibility of our imaginations and conceptualizations, we humans are insatiable creatures. No sooner is one of our desires satisfied than we conceive of another desire—or a better way of satisfying the first desire. Because of human imagination and conceptualization, human desires are endless, and so human dissatisfaction is also without end. What other than an endless, impossible heroic effort could possibly be equal to the protean immensity of our conceptual minds?

We need the impossible idealism of the bodhisattva vows, but we also need to balance that idealism with realism, lest we are overcome with fantasy and fanaticism, as we so easily can be. Realism is the opposite of idealism: devotion to what is rather than to what should or might be. Without impossible idealism we would always be selling ourselves short and so would never be able to find satisfaction. But if we were only impossibly idealistic, we would soar off into the heavens, losing our place on earth, and become feckless dreamers or, worse, ruthless tyrants for whom the end of pursuing our vow justifies all means. So we need to balance idealism with realism, giving our best attention not only to what could or should be but also, with a gentle honesty, to what actually is.

Suppose our vow is a personal one: for instance, to live with integrity and kindness. We aim for that in everything we do, we take our vow seriously, and we make efforts in that direction and are willing to keep up these efforts no matter how difficult it may be. But we also see clearly how we actually are now—we are not always so kind, not always so straightforward, and in fact we often forget our vow entirely! But that's all right. We can be patient with ourselves. Our realism about how we are is no cause for despair. Naturally we are not yet where we want to be. Naturally we have all sorts of doubts and imperfections. We probably always will. The journey is long, but there's no rush. Each day's progress starts from where we are—where else could it start from? There is no use wishing it were otherwise. There's an old saying in Zen: if you fall down on the ground, it is the ground you use to get yourself up. The vow uses the ground of our present imperfection and doubt as purchase to establish itself ever more firmly. Each time we acknowledge our limitation and affirm our vow anyway, we strengthen it. It is fine and normal to fall short of our aspirations. How could it be otherwise?

We need to learn what it takes to pursue our vow and how to take care of ourselves in the process so that we don't eat ourselves up with obsession or burnout. Bernie certainly did this. He remained faithful to his spiritual practice as a way of keeping his own balance. In establishing Greyston he had to learn how to fund-raise, set up a large social service organization, work with poor people whose culture was quite different from his own, and master local politics. Staying aware of his impossible vow with constant faith, was certainly important, but not enough. He also had to figure out, as all of us need to, what it really takes in practical terms to fulfill our vow as best we can. And he had to be flexible enough to deal with failure and adjust his plans when they didn't work and change direction when circumstances called for it.

So idealism and realism are not incompatible. In fact, they depend on each other. How can we hold the vow to be better—as good as we can possibly and impossibly be—without being patient with how we are now? How can we vow to change the world unless we know the world, know how to work in it as it actually is, and can take care of ourselves in the process?

To live with complete dedication to our vows doesn't require that we give up all personal enjoyment or self-interest, or that we live grimly and desperately, devoted solely to our cause, with no sense of play. The vowing life has plenty of enjoyment in it. But when we practice vowing, we aren't seeking pleasure or joy for its own sake—that's not our goal or motivation. Like Abraham, we trust that we will find all that we really need through following our vow.

I know many monastics who have taken solemn vows of poverty, stability, obedience, and chastity. To most of us such vows seem forbiddingly austere. Although we might respect them, we certainly don't see them as the path to a joyful life. And yet, many of the monastics I know are joyful people, and both interesting and interested. One of them, the Benedictine monk Brother David Steindl-Rast, has spent most of his life traveling all over the world, sharing his spiritual life not only with Catholic lay and monastic practitioners in the West, but also with people of different faiths and cultural backgrounds. He has practiced in many different spiritual centers, even spending time living in our Zen monastery, Tassajara. His long life has been full of diverse adventures and friendships. Brother David took his monastic vows more than fifty years ago; I am sure that at the time he never imagined that his life would turn out as it did. It seems quite counterintuitive that vows of stability, chastity, obedience, and poverty would lead to such a life, but Brother David, always true to his vow, found it quite unexpectedly to be so.

Although most of us will never take monastic vows or other formal religious vows (other than, perhaps, marriage vows), we respect the values of faithfulness and commitment that lie at the heart of vowing. Most of us hold these values in our relationships and in our personal lives. Every commitment, every act of faithfulness, and certainly every vow is an act of restraint: whatever I choose wholeheartedly (and vowing is nothing if not wholehearted) will necessarily entail letting go of that which I haven't chosen. This requirement seems like a limitation, and indeed in this era of choice and possibility people seem unwilling or unable to make commitments because of it. Many of us imagine that our limitless potential will be diminished by any committed choice we may make.

This is true of all of us, but perhaps especially of young people. When you're young, you feel the immense expansiveness of the unlived life yet ahead, the imaginary, limitless, undefined, and undisclosed possible life. But I sometimes wonder whether any of us, at any age, have really given up our youthful dreams of a colorful and exciting life. Maybe we've just stored them away in the deep drawers of our heart's attic and bring them out now and then in our quiet daydream hours. Maybe, holding on to these possibilities, we have always held ourselves in reserve, not giving ourselves fully to what our lives have become. To live a life of vowing is to offer ourselves completely to our lives, with nothing held back.

Philip Whalen, one of the original Beat poets, was one of the most important mentors and friends in my life. A large bearded man and a voracious reader, he made a vow to poetry early in his life. Specifically, he vowed to carry on with writing as his sole and full-time occupation no matter what it cost him. Outwardly this vow cost him quite a bit. He was often poor to the point of being destitute, and sometimes he was lonely, lost, and in despair. I am sure that many of his friends criticized him for not having a career or livelihood. Eventually the passion of his vow to poetry met his faith in the practice of Buddhism, and he came to the Zen Center, where he ordained as a priest, and this is how I got to know him.

Externally Philip's life was quite plain, poor, and uneventful. He had few possessions, hardly ever traveled, and became more and more quiet as he got older. In the end, when his eyesight failed him, he even gave up poetry—or at least the writing and reading of it. But his inner life remained full, extravagant and imaginative. This anyone could see from reading his poems. Even after he stopped writing, I saw it in his conversation, in the style and attitude he kept at the heart of all aspects of his living. When he died recently, his many friends from all over the country and the world paid tribute to him. His vow, even accounting for all the limitations it put on his life, turned out in the end to have given him a life that was expansive and full of love.

There is a discipline at the heart of Philip's life and Brother David's life. Philip's discipline was his ongoing writing of poetry as well as his Zen meditation practice, to which he was completely faithful. For Brother David, the life of prayer and contemplation remains a discipline still. Vowing requires some form of discipline if it is to be sustained. Discipline is a way of reinforcing our intention and passion to live a wider life. If we don't back up these vows with concrete and regular practice, they grow stale and eventually fade away.

It also helps to do such practice in the midst of a community so that we can find encouragement and support to carry on with what we know is the right thing to do, even though sometimes our energy or commitment may flag. When that happens, the others in our community pick us up and help us along—and we do the same for them. This is why religious practice over the millennia in all traditions has been communal and includes observances to be carried out at appointed times of the day, week, month, and year.

Although religious traditions are by no means the only examples we have of the vowing life, it is certainly true that vowing and the establishment of a life that supports vowing have been religion's central offerings. The world's great religious traditions are alive and well, and they are still capable of supporting us in our vows. But it may be that these traditions, in and of themselves, no longer provide enough support. We have become habituated to them by long cultural tradition; for many people, religious tradition has become time-worn and less useful in the effort to awaken and sustain their true vows. This is not to say that the great traditions can't wake us up, but rather that to do so they need to be constantly renewed.

For the last several years I have been practicing Zen beyond the San Francisco Zen Center temples, where I lived for so long and served as abbot. As a way of testing and extending my vows, I founded, with some friends, an organization called the Everyday Zen Foundation. It was our idea to see whether it is possible for the powerful sense of vow as practice to be effective for ordinary people in the everyday world. We can't all be Roshi Bernies or Brother Davids. We can't all take religious orders and live in monasteries or Zen centers where our vows are reinforced on a daily basis. Is there a way to live our vowing in our ordinary worldly lives as we find them?

So far we have been finding that there is a way. Most of the students of Everyday Zen find tremendous fulfillment in their spouses and children, and many are pursuing important and useful careers. But they come seeking, in addition to satisfying careers and family lives, a sense of vowing. Many of them have been able to find it by engaging in daily meditation practice at home, attending weekly and monthly meetings with others to share practice and teachings, and most important of all, using all these things to find and sustain within themselves the vow that has always been there.

The students of Everyday Zen aspire to be bodhisattvas— saving all beings, ending all confusion, mastering all wisdoms. I think they are succeeding in this, impossible though it may sound. One person does it by working for the United Nations Health Organization and traveling all over the world training doctors in the treatment of AIDS. One person does it through medical research to find cures for rheumatism and Parkinson's disease. Another does it through her psychotherapy work with children who have suffered serious illness, as she did herself when she was a child. Someone else teaches meditation to the prisoners of San Quentin; still another takes care of dying people as a hospice nurse. Another devotes herself to the care of her severely disabled son. Not all manifest the bodhisattva spirit in ways that appear so overtly altruistic—financial advisors, business executives, ordinary blue- and white-collar workers of every kind also find ways to express their practice through their work. One student of Everyday Zen has a unique approach: he has undertaken to get the world dancing by renting and installing dance floors all over the West Coast and as far away as Texas! Together we encourage each other to see that these and other methods—in combination with our meditation practice and the cultivation of our inner feeling of kindness and honesty—can be skillful means of serving and strengthening our path of vowing, which is endlessly and gloriously unfulfillable and crucially necessary.

Making our vows explicit and clear helps us to strengthen them. This can be done through ceremonies of vowing (as Tony wanted to do, and as many students of Zen do) or in a more personal way by reflecting on your own vows for a long time until they become formed into words within your heart. I have often advised students to write down these words and carefully compose phrases that express their feeling and sound like intentions they can live by. Some students aspire to have a profound effect on the world. But most find their vows to be about inner work, about ways of living or feeling. Some may write words like, "I vow to live in kindness," or, "I vow to listen, to let go of self-interest, to be the kind of parent to my children my parents could not be to me." Such a vow could be the product of many hours of tearful reflection and gathering determination. You can place written vows like these on a personal home altar so that they become a daily inspiration and reminder for your practice. You can also repeat them during your meditation or prayer, or even as you take a moment for reflection during any part of your day.

Sometimes sharing our vows with others helps to strengthen them. In our Everyday Zen meetings we have sometimes given up the formal question-and-answer periods that are customary in Zen practice in favor of intimate small group discussion periods in which we share with each other our deepest explorations and commitments. In this way we hear other people's vows in the making, and their struggles and successes can inspire our own, giving us increased confidence that it really is possible to live a life of vowing.

Vowing is like walking toward the horizon: you know where you are headed, you can see the destination brightly up ahead, and you keep on going toward it with enthusiasm even though you never arrive there. As the Talmud says, "It is not for you to complete the task. But neither are you to ignore it."

Eight

C O N D U C T

IN CLASSICAL BUDDHISM, AS IN ALL RELIGIOUS TRADITIONS, the spiritual life is seen as all-encompassing, embracing the whole of a person's life. All our conduct, all our thought and feeling, all our relationships, encounters, and decisions are part of the path. If we take the spiritual life to be the fullness of human maturity, as I believe it is, then spiritual practice can't be something merely private and personal, limited only to a separate and special part of life.

In Buddhism spiritual practice is likened to a tripod whose three balanced legs hold a bowl steady and firm. These legs are the three practices of ethical conduct, meditation, and wisdom. They work together, each one helping to support the other two. Although it is easy enough to sit down on a cushion, you can't really practice meditation without practicing right conduct. If your actions are thoughtless and crooked, your meditation will reflect this, and calm concentration will be hard to achieve. But if you go on with meditation anyway, you'll begin to see the shadows that your conduct is casting on your mind and heart. You'll feel these shadows as unpleasant and undesirable, and you'll want to change your way of life. When you do, your meditation will deepen, becoming calmer, and some insight will come. You'll have fewer illusions about yourself and will be able to appreciate yourself as you really are. Accepting yourself realistically, in turn, will give you more energy for your meditation practice. It will become clear to you that practicing ethical conduct is necessary because it directly affects every thought and action, small and large. In this way meditation, ethical conduct, and wisdom refine, deepen, and balance each other, until little by little the vessel of your life stands strong.

In Zen the practice of ethical conduct is both beginning and advanced practice. While new students are encouraged to conduct themselves straightforwardly in order to learn the practice, experienced students know that their conduct is the expression of their practice in the world—the most difficult accomplishment of all. In some schools of Zen the koans that come at the very end of the long course of study involve a thorough penetration of the ethical precepts, which are seen now not as simple moral rules but as profound spiritual truths. In our school of Zen, which does not have a systematic curriculum of koan study, precept study that includes the deepest insights of our teaching lineage is offered at the very end of formal training. (Precepts are studied at the beginning and middle of practice as well.)

Zen practice has two parts—sitting down and getting up. When we sit down, we calm, clear, and illuminate the mind. When we get up, we live our life in this world as an extension and expression of the beauty of our sitting. Sitting down and getting up together comprise a full and mature human being, one who is receptive and open but also responsible and committed.

Although we recognize the importance of ethical conduct and believe we know the difference between right and wrong, how much thought have we really given to what right and wrong mean in this complicated world? Living an ethical life is not a simple matter. In addition to some understanding of the foundations of morality, living ethically takes a degree of courage and awareness that few of us have taken the time to develop. Have we considered ethical conduct as an active, thoughtful, challenging, and ongoing practice?

It would be comforting to think that ethical conduct can be clearly codified, that it is founded on certainties, and that to do good is simply to conform to these certainties. Unfortunately, this isn't so. Life is full of gray areas, and we are full of unexamined motivations and self-deceptions. We are much better off when we admit this and are willing to look at our conduct honestly, with as much awareness as possible of our real motivations and the consequences of our actions. The practice of ethical conduct requires that much honesty and awareness, for it is an ongoing exploration, a constant steering of a moral course that depends on accurate information, not theory and bluster. Fixed moral codes are always theoretical. They are vastly subject to interpretation, since no ethical norm can ever take into account all of life's subtlety and complexity. Instead of focusing our effort on such norms, we need to pay more attention to what we feel, what others feel, and what actually happens.

Given this indeterminacy (and it is already a mark of maturity to accept it, for only the immature hold fast to certainties), it makes sense that in practicing ethical conduct we are going to make mistakes, and plenty of them. We steer our boat by paying attention to the rocks and shoals. We know that once in a while, because the rocks are hidden, or because we weren't watching, we are going to hit one, and that sometimes this is the only way to find out that it is there. Mistakes are not tragedies. Without them there's no learning or growth. It is precisely our moral mistakes, much more than our moral victories, that deepen our sense of what ethical conduct is. Our mistakes mature us and temper us; they fire us like strong pottery.

Of course, this does not mean that we are casual about our mistakes, or that we don't try to avoid them. A mistake that we don't care about is a mistake we haven't noticed, a mistake we haven't learned from yet. We need to care deeply about our mistakes and to have sincerely terrible feelings about them—remorse, embarrassment, shame.

If the powerful negativity of a really bad mistake doesn't come home to you, if it never sears your soul, then that mistake has been useless to you; it will not serve to temper and tenderize your heart. Once you fully feel remorse for your mistake, you are ready to confess it, and then to forgive yourself. This process might take a good deal of time. Some really terrible mistakes may need to stay buried for many years, since feeling them might be too painful, at least for a while. But most of the time we eventually do come to feel the effects of our mistakes, and we find a way to forgive ourselves and move on—a little wiser and clearer about where we are going and what we need to watch out for.

Our mistakes are painful not only because they make us feel bad, but because they have consequences. As responsible people, we want to accept those consequences and not try to escape them. When we make a mistake, we admit it not only to ourselves but to others. We pay the price for it by apologizing to whomever we might have hurt and making all possible amends. We also resolve not to make the same mistake again; and we take steps in our lives to make sure we are able to stand by that resolve. If we make the same mistake over and over again we haven't really owned the mistake, been truly aware of it, forgiven ourselves for it, and so been changed by it. We have just been playing out the terrible consequences of our continuing blindness—and in fact reinforcing it.

For some of us the practice of ethical conduct takes us through some pretty rough and narrow passages, and we crash and founder disastrously for some time. We may have to nearly drown before we are ready to be aware enough to forgive ourselves. We may have to hit bottom before we can float up. The Talmud tells the story of Eliezar ben Durdia, an awful sinner who sinned constantly and paid no attention to what he was doing. His favorite sin was fornication. One day a prostitute he was with turned to him, looked him in the eye, and said, "You will never be forgiven for this!" Ben Durdia was deeply affected. He leapt up, ran outside, and threw himself down on the ground, tearing his clothes, throwing ashes on himself, and weeping uncontrollably. He cried out to the earth to help him, but the earth would not help him. He cried out to the sky to help him, but the sky would not help him. He cried out to the planets and the stars, but they were totally indifferent. So he just sat there wailing for a very long time. Finally a voice out of the heavens said to him, "You have won life everlasting." When the rabbis heard about this, they were furious: they had never heard a voice come out of the heavens promising *them* life everlasting. They who had worked so hard to be good, and were so good, had never received the reward that this miserable sinner received.

Forgiveness for our mistakes is always possible once we start to pay attention to what we have been doing, no matter how long it takes us. And sometimes, as this story shows, a person who has been unaware for a long time and finally comes to suffer horribly for it finds a deeper, more sudden, and more moving redemption than the rest of us.

If there are no fixed moral standards we can refer to in all circumstances, and if mistakes are not only inevitable but even useful, is there no moral compass? Is ethical conduct a matter of trial and error—with the emphasis on error? Is our own eventual guilt and remorse following wrong actions the only way we have of steering our conduct?

I believe there is indeed a moral compass, one that all religious traditions recognize. The needle of that compass is kindness, simple human kindness. I am in agreement with the Dalai Lama who says, "My religion is kindness."

Bodhisattvas build their practice of ethical conduct on a vision of the world's interconnectedness. They see with their wisdom eye of meditative insight that the world is empty of separation, boundary, and cramped limitation and that it is full of connection, merging, warmth, and embrace. The clear consequence of this profound spiritual experience is a feeling of kindness. Since we are all so closely related, all of us articulations of one body, one soul, how could we not have affection for each other? More than a warm fuzzy sentiment, kindness is the natural and powerful urge that wells up inside us when our vision of reality is deep and clear.

We all recognize kindness when we see it or feel it, and we all honor it and are moved by it. We don't need to be convinced. The fact that we are capable of kindness, of a pure and unselfconscious concern for others, is the center of our practice of right conduct. We can rely on kindness and on our good heart to show us how to act in the world. Although we may not always know whether a particular action is good or bad, whether it will lead to well-being or suffering, we can pay attention to our motivation, moving it in the direction of our natural kindness whenever possible. When this is not possible—when we find that we can't shake our jealousy, anger, fear, greed, or aggression—we can at least admit this and recognize that these feelings are not what we affirm, not what we want to use as a basis for our actions.

In one of the many sutras in which he speaks of right conduct, the Maha Assapura Sutra, the Buddha says, "We will not praise ourselves and disparage others on account of our purified conduct." A crucial aspect of our practice of ethical conduct is that we refrain from cheering about our moral successes and grumbling about others' moral failures.

The Rule of Saint Benedict, the fifth-century monastic code that still governs all Christian monasteries, makes much of the virtue of humility, which is considered the cornerstone of the religious life. To be humble is to be willing to make efforts toward right conduct without measuring our success. The point isn't to see ourselves as good or bad, worthy or unworthy. The point is to go on doing our best to be kind in our actions and clear about our intentions.

Hui Neng, the Sixth Ancestor of Zen, says, "I see and I don't see." When someone asked him what he meant by this, he said, "I see my own faults, but I don't see the faults of others." We are most thoroughly humble when we literally do not see the faults of others. This doesn't mean that we are fools who don't recognize wrong action when we see it—and if necessary, try to prevent it—but rather that we do this with passion for the good, not with a sense of judging or criticizing others. Even when circumstances dictate that we criticize others, we try to do so with a generous, nonblaming spirit.

In particle physics the search for the irreducible core of matter yields only a seemingly endless proliferation of parts. The more closely you look at the parts, the less easily they can be found—they seem to be indeterminate and relative to the very act of your looking. While on a gross level we can distinguish one thing from another, on a refined level no thing is actually findable. Similarly, the more closely you look into your own conduct and the conduct of others, the less you will find a "me" to be right or a "you" to be wrong, and the less you will find a "right" or a "wrong," a "good" or a "bad." There is only the wide, true, and deep effort to be effectively kind beyond moral judgment or discrimination.

Humility and kindness are good flashlights for illuminating the path of ethical conduct. But even if we are genuinely humble and perfectly kind, we don't necessarily know what to do in a given situation. We also need practical path-finding skills to help us see which way to go. Bodhisattvas are always working to develop this capacity to know what is needed in any given situation. Each situation is unique. What is right one moment may be entirely wrong the next. Ethical conduct is a wonderfully complex dance; in addition to a kind and humble heart, it takes intelligence, experience, feeling, common sense, and a willingness to start fresh each time.

When Suzuki Roshi, the founder of our Zen lineage in America, was a young disciple, he had the job of bringing tea to his master. The first time he did this he filled the cup half full, as is usually done with handleless Japanese teacups (so that the cup won't be too hot to hold). But his master scolded him harshly: regardless of custom, he wanted the teacup filled to the brim. So Suzuki learned to pour tea in this way. One day a guest came to the temple, and Suzuki served the tea as he had been taught. Again he was scolded bitterly—a teacup should be filled only half full, he was told. Do you want our guest to burn her fingers?

Sometimes full, sometimes half full, depending on the circumstances. Skill is the sensitivity and readiness to discern what's right in the circumstances that are arising just now.

Ethical conduct requires such skill, as well as kindness, flexibility, humility, and a powerful appreciation of life's complexity and fullness. Because of this, the practice of ethical conduct can be seen as the pinnacle of the spiritual life. Through it we express and live what we have learned and become. The practice of ethical conduct is both a tool for the development of our maturity and the very expression of that maturity, which is neither a state of mind nor an accomplishment, but an ongoing path toward understanding that is reflective as well as active. To be truly mature is to always make the effort to conduct and express ourselves with kindness, clarity, wisdom, and beauty. In this sense, the practice of ethical conduct is fundamental to our maturity. All the other practices that we have discussed support, deepen, and strengthen it.

THE SIXTEEN BODHISATTVA PRECEPTS

In Zen the practice of ethical conduct is summarized in the sixteen bodhisattva precepts. Though these precepts are said to describe most profoundly—and also quite practically—the way a mature person conducts himself or herself, they are not understood as a fixed code of conduct. Instead, they are approached as koans—as objects for contemplation and clarification through the lessons of our lives. Students work on the precepts one or several at a time—or sometimes all at once—using them as points of illumination to shed light on aspects of conduct. Precepts are understood as practices.

The sixteen precepts constitute the vows that Tony had decided to take, and they formed the basis of the discussion of ethical conduct that went on for some time in our group meetings.

The sixteen precepts begin with the ancient Buddhist formula of taking refuge in what's traditionally called the Triple Treasure of Buddha, Dharma, and Sangha:

1. I take refuge in Buddha (the principle of enlightenment within).

2. I take refuge in dharma (the enlightened way of understanding and living).

3. I take refuge in sangha (the community of all beings).

After these come the three "pure" precepts:

1. I vow to avoid all action that creates suffering.

2. I vow to do all action that creates true happiness.

3. I vow to act with others always in mind.

Next come the ten "grave" precepts of conduct, which can be stated in both negative and positive form—as what to do and what not to do:

1. Not to kill but to nurture life.

2. Not to steal but to receive what is offered as a gift.

3. Not to misuse sexuality but to be caring and faithful in intimate relationships.

4. Not to lie but to be truthful.

5. Not to intoxicate with substances or doctrines but to promote clarity and awareness.

6. Not to speak of others' faults but to speak out of loving-kindness.

7. Not to praise self at the expense of others but to be modest.

8. Not to be possessive of anything but to be generous.

9. Not to harbor anger but to forgive.

10. Not to do anything to diminish the Triple Treasure but to support and nurture it.

(There are many ways of stating the precepts. The above is my favorite version.)

The sixteen precepts evoke the depth and power of human responsibility. The more thoughtful we are about our life, and the more we deepen our thoughtfulness through our spiritual practice, the more we see that the scope of our life is wider than we ever imagined. All our actions have effects that spread subtly throughout the world. This means that all of our actions, even the seemingly inconsequential ones, have huge implications. We practice the sixteen precepts with the understanding that we are responsible for the whole world and capable of redeeming the whole world through our acts. In Zen there's an old saying that expresses this: "When you pick up one piece of dust, the entire world comes with it." All our actions, however small they may seem, can have wondrous effects, if only we are wholehearted enough in our practice of ethical conduct.

This same point is made in Judaism's Hasidic teachings (and, I am sure, in the mystical teachings of all religious traditions). It seems that the Baal Shem Tov, the eighteenth-century founder of the Hasidic movement, was unmatched in the fervor of his prayer. He sometimes prayed with such passion that he would fall ill, and it was only the encouragement of his disciples, who loved him dearly and feared for his well-being, that kept him in this world. The Baal Shem loved God very much, but the real reason for his passionate prayer was that he felt personally responsible for the whole world. He felt as if his prayers, and his alone, were all that kept the evil and confusion of the world from inundating humankind.

I am sure that the Baal Shem realized that the world would not fall apart if he forgot to pray for one day, and yet, at the same time his feeling of ultimate responsibility was quite real to him, and it must have given his prayer a power that helped him to live a life of depth and seriousness. We are all like the Baal Shem: the whole world really does depend on the awareness and good conduct of each one of us.

The Triple Treasure

The first three of the sixteen precepts are the Triple Treasure—taking refuge in Buddha, dharma, and sangha. The word *refuge* means, literally, to fly back, to return, as a bird flies home to her nest. To take refuge in the Triple Treasure is to return to our own real nature as conscious human beings who were born with, and have never ceased to possess (however much we may have forgotten it) open minds and tender hearts.

Returning to Buddha is acknowledging that our inmost nature is the nature of awareness, of awakening—that awareness is the root of our consciousness and awakening is the birthright of our life. Returning to dharma is acknowledging that we have always longed to understand life in accord with our open mind and tender heart, and that we have always wanted to live lives based on that understanding. Returning to sangha is acknowledging that we have always been a part of the interconnected network of all beings—who cannot be separated from one another any more than water can be separated from water or sky from sky—and that we want to embrace that fabric of connection fully, and be embraced by it, living in concert with all that is.

If we could fully and completely take refuge in the Triple Treasure, if these acknowledgments could be entirely incorporated into our understanding and living, then the spiritual path would be complete, and we would surely take our places immediately as mature and awakened human beings. There would be no need to take up the study and practice of the other precepts—we would already be them, and our conduct would naturally flow from our being.

But none of us has fully and completely taken refuge; none of us has completely returned to the fullness of our human potential. The first three precepts are expressions of our intention and our commitment to a way of life and action. They are always, for any of us, a work in progress, a path, a hope, the endless effort we want to make.

The Pure Precepts

The next three precepts, the "pure" precepts, are less poetic and less metaphysical than the Triple Treasure. Coming down from the lofty heights of the purity of the awakened open heart, we practice these precepts to affirm that on the human plane on which we are born and die there are wholesome and unwholesome actions, and wholesome and unwholesome consequences. There is good and bad, as we would say in plain English.

The first pure precept commits us to avoiding unwholesome action that will increase suffering; we restrain ourselves from doing or saying—even, as much as possible, from thinking—things that will cause harm. The second pure precept comes at conduct from the opposite angle: we pledge ourselves not only to practice restraint and neutrality but beyond this to discover and do that which is wholesome and promotes not a superficial but a lasting happiness. The third pure precept considers our motivation for following the first two: it commits us to act to avoid suffering and to promote happiness unselfishly in order to benefit others, not only ourselves. This is not conventional altruism. The Triple Treasure shows us that when we return to our own true nature, the benefit and happiness of others is none other than our own benefit and happiness.

The Grave Precepts

The final ten precepts are called the "grave" precepts, for they are the most gravity-laden, the most embedded within the weightiness of the relative world. Although the ten precepts are also light and joyful, just as the ordinary world is light and joyful when seen with the spiritual eye, they represent the issues we must grapple with as we get down to the real business of manifesting our maturity in the world. The ten precepts take us beyond the soaring insight of the Triple Treasure and the high good intentions of the pure precepts to what we do and don't do in the daily course of living.

The First Grave Precept: Not to Kill but to Nurture Life

On the surface, this precept seems quite simple to keep. The murderers among us are vastly in the minority; for most of us it is fairly easy to restrain ourselves from acting on the violent impulses that now and then arise. But as we will see with all ten of the grave precepts, looking a bit deeper always raises many doubts. Maybe we find it easy to refrain from killing our coworkers, spouse, or children when they upset us, but what about killing animals? Do we do that for sport? Maybe not, but do we eat meat or fish? If so, are we participating in killing? Even if we are vegetarians, killing is still involved in our consuming. Maybe we don't think a vegetable minds being harvested, but what about the insects and animals that are inevitably killed in the process of growing food, no matter how carefully we do it?

I remember a Zen talk given at our temple by the priest who at the time was in charge of our fifteen-acre farm. Speaking about this precept of nonkilling, he told us about all the killing that he had done that very day as he drove his mower through a thick field of cover crop—the birds' nests, snakes, and field mice that he had unintentionally sliced in half, all in the service of producing our good organic produce. No matter how pure we are trying to be, we certainly participate in some killing if we eat to satisfy our appetites and preserve our lives.

Beyond this, do we pay our taxes and enjoy the benefits of living under a government that might kill people in war or, through neglect or ignorance in its policies, kill the poor and homeless? I know that in San Francisco scores of people die on the streets each year for lack of housing and medical care because the local, state, and national governments have decided to spend funds that might have helped them on other projects.

Beyond literal, physical killing, what about killing the spirit, killing the heart—forms of violence that might be just as bad, if not sometimes worse? Not killing means affirming life, nurturing and respecting life. Do we really practice that? Or are we often thoughtless about how we talk to and view others, treating them dismissively or disrespectfully because we are too cranky or tired to do otherwise? Or perhaps because we view them as enemies or rivals and feel the need to cut them down to size? Or simply because they have hurt our feelings and we want to retaliate?

To nurture life requires that we cultivate an attitude of respect for other living beings, not because there is anything special about them, but simply because they *are* living beings and therefore part of the network of life. For many of us, affection for plants and animals and for the earth comes easily enough. But when it comes to nurturing other people, we are not so sanguine.

In classical Buddhism there is a wonderful practice for cultivating the nurturing heart called sympathetic joy: imagine that the success or benefit that someone else is enjoying is also your own success or benefit. When someone wins, even if they have defeated you in the process, rather than saying, "What about me?" you train yourself to say, "How wonderful; this joy is mine also." Look for opportunities to replace your habitual way of thinking with the discipline of thinking in this new way. If you take on the practice of sympathetic joy with diligence, a sense of participation with people will replace your former feeling of wariness. You will become much more capable of nurturing life, and less apt to want to diminish it.

The Second Grave Precept: Not to Steal but to Receive What Is Offered As a Gift

Again, this precept seems easy. You haven't robbed a store lately, and you have no plans to do so. Neither have you embezzled, committed credit card fraud, or shoplifted. If you don't go to an office every day, you can't steal paper clips and legal pads. But even if you do lift something once in a while—well, isn't that just something minor, hardly even worth mentioning?

When it comes to stealing, where do we draw the line? If you use more than your share of this world's resources, is that stealing? If you profit from a stock that goes up owing to shady dealing or unfair advantage, is that stealing? Suppose you simply waste too much of your wealth or live too high off the hog instead of giving your money to causes that support the needy. Are you stealing from them? What about tax avoidance? You can do your best not to steal in any way that you can see, but you may be stealing in unseen ways. How much responsibility do you bear for that?

There are also many harmful forms of stealing that have nothing to do with material things. What about stealing our own or others' precious time with trivial or harmful pursuits? When we spend too much time fooling around with our computer when we could be helping out someone, or even doing something to preserve and enhance our own lives, maybe we are stealing from them or from ourselves. What about our human relationships—do we give as much as we get? If people pursue friendships with us because they are after our business or our money or our ability to introduce them to someone we know whom they want to meet, we usually have the feeling that they are stealing something from us. Do they feel this, too?

The root cause of stealing is probably the feeling that we are not getting enough, that others are getting more than we are, or that we are afraid somehow that unless we look out for ourselves aggressively no one else will. If we steal, however unconsciously, it must be because we feel separate from the world and beset by it. The practice of generosity is a good way to counteract whatever tendency to stealing we might have. To practice generosity is to make a conscious effort to give away whatever we can—money, time, food, feeling—as a way of realizing that generosity is perfectly safe and it's even a relief to give things away. Giving to others doesn't diminish us, it expands us—our hearts and minds open more widely, and we relax.

For some, generosity comes naturally, but others have to work hard at it. Even the naturally generous can practice generosity further, however, for generosity can be expanded without limit. There is no limit to how much you can give inside.

Generosity is a factor in all human encounters. There is always the choice: Am I going to share myself with this person, or will I hold back? Holding back may seem less bothersome, but it will have a shrinking effect on the spirit, making you a smaller and more isolated person.

Generosity also extends to our willingness to share power. Having lived for many years in a Zen community full of good and well-intentioned people, I know that even the best of us can have trouble sharing power honestly. There is probably no way to avoid clashing over power issues, for in the end our struggles over power are struggles about identity. We identify with a position, person, or view and so feel that an opposing position, person, or view threatens us to the very core of who we are. It's difficult to be generous with someone who opposes your view or is at odds with someone you like. And yet, not being generous at times like these only increases the potential for trouble and conflict.

A Greenpeace worker once told me about her efforts to negotiate a coastal protection agreement with a large logging company in the Pacific Northwest. As the negotiations proceeded, the increasing intransigence of the logging company spokespeople made the Greenpeace negotiators feel more and more entrenched in their own views. Finally, the Greenpeace people realized that this total lack of mutual regard was going to kill off the discussions—and therefore the chance to improve the condition of the coastline. So they decided to employ what they called "the love strategy." They worked at developing generous feelings for the logging negotiators and at creating expansiveness in their feelings and views instead of the smallness and stinginess they had been experiencing. In the end this strategy worked: the Greenpeace negotiators reached an agreement that they felt good about.

The positive side of nonstealing is accepting whatever we

receive as a gift. Rather than thinking we deserve what we get, or have earned it, we let go of any feeling of entitlement and are grateful for what comes to us, as if it were freely given to us by a beneficent universe. This feeling of gratitude for everything may be the fullest expression of the understanding of this precept.

It's not easy to cultivate gratitude in the world we live in: everything seems to be tagged to a bottom line, and even intangibles are viewed in terms of exchange, as income balanced by expense. It is possible, however, to overcome the prevalent attitude. Years ago when I worked as a plant nurseryman and received a monthly check for my services, I remember thinking one month that I was being paid very little. Could my time really be worth such a small number of dollars? I decided to consider how much I thought my time was really worth. It didn't take me long to see that my rate of compensation was very far below the value that I placed on my own time. I thought about the per-hour dollar value of my time: it seemed to me that my time was a rare and extremely valuable commodity, precious almost beyond measure considering that each moment of my life, once gone, could never be recouped. I realized that no one could afford to pay me what my time was actually worth. So I decided to consider myself a wealthy person, and to imagine that I was working for free, simply donating my labor. When my check came at the end of the month, I regarded it as a donation, a gift freely given. Since then I have always applied this practice of working for nothing, receiving my compensation as if it were a gift.

The Third Grave Precept: Not to Misuse Sexuality but to Be Caring and Faithful in Intimate Relationships

This is a difficult precept, for when it comes to sexuality, very few of us are completely clear. Our sexuality is deeply rooted in our hearts, and there is always more to it than meets the eye. As a spiritual teacher, I have often been asked to bear witness to the private lives of others and so have seen many people fall prey to their hidden sexual needs and desires in ways that have caused great suffering. Certainly we want the maturing of our spiritual lives to open us to love. But how do we distinguish between the wholesome love between spiritual friends, and the neediness and inner pressure that can lead to self-deception and sexual disaster?

I am amazed at sexuality's power, and at our fascination with it—both far out of proportion to the amount of time we actually spend directly indulging in sexual activity. The realm of sexuality can have disturbing inner reverberations at times: it awakens not only our need for pleasure and fulfillment but also our senses of shame, inadequacy, identity, fear, aggression, obsession. Sexuality is also a way to transcend the desert island of the isolated self and join in some profound way with the life of another. Sexuality holds the promise of self-transcendence, of self-surrender. Are we ready for this? Are we whole enough to endure it? For some the sexual quest is a spiritual journey that can be deeply satisfying as almost nothing else in our life is.

Sexuality also has the power to hurt us as almost nothing else can. Our stability and tranquillity can suddenly be upset—much to our shock and utter surprise—by the strength of sexual feelings that rise up fiercely out of nowhere, compelling us to deeds we never thought we'd do. We have all seen this happen to others if not to ourselves, and certainly we are made aware of it almost constantly in the movies, on television, in magazines, and in books. Even more disturbing is the rape, incest, child abuse, and sexual debasement of all kinds that we now know, after generations of cover-up, to be commonplace. No human tragedy evokes as emotional a response as sexual crimes, which occur everywhere, even within our churches, schools, professions, and civic organizations. And then there are the less dramatic but almost countless ways in which we hurt each other every day with our sexual advances and suggestions—a boss's inappropriate joke or touch, a boyfriend's intimidating sexual need, a wife's rejection of an amorous husband, or vice versa, the wolf whistle on the street, the gesture, the stare.

In the face of sexuality's power and complexity, we try to practice this precept as well as we can, making the effort to be caring and faithful in our sexual relationships. Sexual styles and appetites are vastly different within different societies and individuals, and within the same societies or individuals at different times in their development. So it is impossible to say which sexual acts are hurtful or not hurtful—it depends on the people involved. One thing is certain: we must build our intimate relationships on a fierce honesty about our own sexual needs and feelings. Fooling ourselves about them only opens us to confusion that might lead us to commit harmful actions without knowing what we're doing. Being honest about our own sexual vulnerabilities, we know that others must have their vulnerabilities, too. Just as we know that we can be hurt, so we know that others can be hurt, and we're clear that it can't be right to satisfy our sexual needs without considering the needs and feelings of others as much as we consider our own. To do that we need to take on the responsibility of knowing our partner as deeply as we can.

It seems to me that the more we do know and care for the person we are intimate with, the more satisfying and meaningful our sexual relationship will be. While a long-term committed relationship may not be everyone's goal, this ideal does exist in the hearts of many of us, and it is a worthy one. I myself have been happily married for many years, and I have seen the ideal realized in others. For married people, or people who are otherwise explicitly committed to one another, this precept implies a degree of faithfulness and honesty about sexual conduct that both partners agree to and support.

Whether or not a committed sexual relationship is part of our life path, probably no one has gotten very far into adult life without stumbling onto a few sexual side roads and detours. I don't know of anyone who hasn't had some sexual disasters in his or her lifetime—encounters, whether short or long in duration, that in hindsight have evoked feelings of shame or guilt or anger, or that perhaps evoked those feelings even at the time. If we have hurt someone, been hurt by someone, or stupidly allowed ourselves to go on being hurt by someone when we could have or should have prevented it, we need to acknowledge that and heal it if we can. We try to forgive not only the other person but ourselves; that involves stopping the sexual patterns of aggression or passivity or confusion that got us into trouble in the first place. In severe situations, like rape or abuse, it may be the right thing for us to accuse and prosecute the perpetrator and to be moved to do so by our anger and hurt. Still, in the end we need to find a way to forgive, if only to cleanse our own heart.

Buddha and many other religious people throughout the ages have understood this precept about sexual misconduct in a very clear-cut way: engage in no sexual activity at all. The point of this understanding, I believe, is not to label sexuality as inherently evil or antispiritual, but to acknowledge that it is so powerful and difficult to manage that it interferes with a full commitment to the spiritual life. This may be true for some people, but celibacy certainly doesn't solve all sexual problems; it doesn't eliminate sexuality, no matter how much a celibate person might wish this were so. As Freud pointed out long ago, sexuality is everywhere, coloring almost all areas of our lives, whether we are sexually active or not. The monastic commitment to abstain from overt sexuality is not meant to create an asexual or cold lifestyle, but rather to widen sexuality, taking it beyond genital activity with selected partners to warm-hearted relationship with all.

Most of us are not committed celibate monastics. And yet, the fact is that most of us are celibate most of the time. Even if we are sexually active, we spend much of our time interacting with people who are not our sexual partners—and even with our sexual partners we are most of the time not being overtly sexual. If we are sexually inactive, not by choice but by circumstances, then we certainly are celibate in a literal sense. So rather than either being always on the prowl sexually or blocking out our sexuality because it has proven unsuccessful in our lives, why not affirm our temporary celibacy as an opportunity rather than a deprivation and use it to develop a greater warmth and connection to ourselves and the world?

The Fourth Grave Precept: Not to Lie but to Be Truthful
Lying is an unwholesome action that leads to trouble and unhappiness. Internally, lying makes you nervous. With the first lie you begin to spin a web of untruth around yourself, for soon you need a second lie to support the first, and then further lies, until you are confused about what your story is supposed to be. Sooner or later you will feel the sinking feeling of being so bound up in the web of lies that you can't move. Externally, your lies will hurt others, confusing them and diminishing their capacity to trust.

Few of us consider ourselves to be liars, but probably most of us lie inadvertently, through laziness, inattentiveness, exaggeration, or too much attachment to our own point of view. This kind of subtle lying can ruin a relationship—acting like a slow poison, it gradually robs the relationship of its vitality.

Reflecting on this, we may recognize our laxity and try to improve. We find, however, that it's not so simple. The more scrupulously we try to tell the truth, the more we see that truth isn't always such a clear path. As we look more closely at our words, our hearts, our thoughts, our feelings, and our motivations, we become less and less clear about what's true. There's an old Zen saying: "Everything's true, everything's false." The truth (and falsity!) of this statement begins to impress itself on us as we intensify our efforts to be truthful with our words.

It is nearly impossible most of the time to know what's true. Reality is so multifaceted that the truth seems to shift and skip and slide around. In the famous Akira Kurosawa film *Rashomon*, a story is told over and over again, each time from the point of view of a different character. Each telling is quite different from the others, and each seems true. Like a fun house full of mirrors each of which shows a different distortion of the same reality, the film leaves the viewer dazzled and disturbed. Life is like this, too—the more versions of your story you consider, the harder it becomes to find a single truth.

But even supposing you could discover the one view that is true above all others, you'd still have to put that truth into words and communicate it somehow. This raises the question of *how* we speak the truth—skillfully or unskillfully, thoroughly or with only a few details, kindly or not so kindly, at the right time or at the wrong time. In what style and at what pace do we communicate this version of the truth? With what attitude and tone of voice? All of these factors make more of a difference than you might think, not just in style but in substance.

This uncertainty about truth is even more pronounced in the emotional realm. The truth is that we are aware of our feelings only selectively—so much of what motivates us and disturbs or pleases us remains below the surface. The way others see and experience us is often vastly different from the way we see and experience ourselves. Anyone who has ever been immersed in an emotional conversation about feelings and attitudes with an intimate friend knows that emotional truth can be very elusive.

Truth is no easier to find in the public arena, where we are supposed to be dealing with objective facts. Politicians, attorneys, and businesspeople are constantly accusing one another of subverting or obscuring the truth, and it is difficult to evaluate who is right and who is wrong. Facts do not seem to be facts—they are endlessly subject to spin and interpretation. We might well wonder whether there is any such thing as a public truth. And yet, when we hear truth spoken publicly, we feel its power. Speeches by Abraham Lincoln, Martin Luther King Jr., Nelson Mandela, Mahatma Gandhi, Frederick Douglass, or Cesar Chavez still stir us with their truth power.

Public or private, truth-telling does have magical power. Despite the difficulty of finding and proving truth, we all know truth when we hear it because it resonates with our own deep sense of what's right. Like a Mandela or a Gandhi, we, too, through reflection and the courage of our convictions, can go beyond the confusion of our biases to discover what we feel is true and speak it.

Someone who habitually exaggerates and speaks untruthfully out of selfishness, anger, or impetuousness will be known for that. Losing value day by day, his or her words will eventually be discounted. But the person who tries to remain aware of his or her own motivations and desires, and speaks what's true, not to win a point but simply out of concern for what's right, will be heard and respected. This person's words will be healing and effective.

I am fortunate to know many people who practice telling the truth. They are not saints or great leaders but ordinary human beings who have recognized how satisfying it can be to tell the truth. They know that the heart and mind are relieved when we tell the truth rather than speak only out of a guarded self-interest. They practice this precept in both their work lives and their private lives, committing themselves to saying what's true as they honestly see it and feel it, with sensitivity and understanding. One person I know manages to do this in his work as a financial adviser for a large brokerage firm. When he first took on the practice of truth-telling with his clients and coworkers, he feared that it would cost him many accounts, his investment performance would go down, or his coworkers would disapprove. But the opposite has been the case. While his success at work has not increased dramatically, neither has it fallen off, and he has a lot more peace and happiness with what he is doing.

The Fifth Grave Precept: Not to Intoxicate with Substances or Doctrines but to Promote Clarity and Awareness

This precept is usually understood to be about the use of substances like drugs or alcohol, but its practice actually goes much deeper. This precept strikes at the heart of our relationship to what's difficult and unpleasant in our lives. A mature person is patient and steady enough to be able to face what is. He or she knows that trying to escape or avoid unpleasant realities simply doesn't work, for a problem avoided is a problem compounded. Intoxication is an act of avoidance—refusing to face what is by covering it over with something else we hope will be more pleasant. In this sense, almost anything can be an intoxicant—television, music, games, reading, shopping, even relationships, doctrines, or ideologies. Whatever functions in our lives to blunt the force of our awareness, preventing us from experiencing our life as it really is, is an intoxicant.

Intoxication that masks strong, unacknowledged pain in our lives is the most virulent kind, for it easily snowballs, and we find ourselves the victims of a strong compulsion to go on and on with our practice of intoxication until we become dysfunctional. This is the realm of addiction, which is all too common in our time. In Buddhist mythology a being called a hungry ghost dwells in hell and is constantly seeking food and drink. His quest for food is especially desperate and pathetic because his belly is huge and his throat is the size of a needle. No matter how much he stuffs into his mouth, he can never get enough through his throat to satisfy his hunger. Hungry ghosts, constantly ravenous, howl and moan their way through their lives. This painful image fits very well the tragedy of human compulsive desire, which truly is a hell realm. No one would ever enter it consciously.

Intoxication is also a confused attempt to cope with our deep-seated and unlimited human desires. We want so much, consciously and unconsciously: inner qualities like happiness, love, and satisfaction, and outer acquisitions like money, property, power, beauty, and youthfulness. Most of us find the pressure of these desires too much to bear, so we try not to notice them. We may drink a bit too much alcohol every evening—it is so much simpler than making the effort to find the peace we seek. Instead of admitting our loneliness and trying to do something about it, we may watch a lot of television or shop more than we need to or can afford. Rather than confronting the energies inside us, which might liven us up if only we could find a way to deal with them, we dull ourselves with intoxicants.

We all understand the tragedy of addiction, and most of us avoid the more serious forms. But how many of us depend on one form of intoxication or another just to get through the unhappiness and confusion of our days? Do we know the difference between relaxation and running away?

How can we work with our desire and our pain? The positive side of this precept gives us a way—the practice of awareness. Leaving off distraction and avoidance, we try to face what really is: our disappointments, our stresses, our pain, our desire. Everything we feel and experience in our lives is our gift and our responsibility. We have to find a way to meet it, live with it, and give it room to transform. Rather than using distraction to leap over our feelings, we practice staying with them, turning toward them, facing them, until they change, as all things do if we allow them to. When we practice this way, we find that even our worst problems can be useful. We can learn from them, bringing depth and liberation to our lives. Even our wild desires can be tamed and give us pleasure in ways that don't hurt us or anyone else. Doing this work of transformation does take some kind of spiritual discipline, like meditation or prayer and the support of others who are committed to doing the same work. But discipline can be developed and support can be found; the work can be done.

The Sixth Grave Precept: Not to Speak of Other's Faults but to Speak out of Loving-Kindness

Talk is cheap, as the saying goes, because words are plentiful. We won't run out. But talk is also precious: what we say to and about others matters a great deal, and whether or not they say so or even know it, people are hurt by our careless words, just as they are helped by our inspired or kind words.

Because we have critical intelligence, we can't help but evaluate others—our minds simply function this way—and then naturally we speak about the mistakes and shortcomings we see. It seems that this is unavoidable, that if we took a pledge never to speak about the faults of others, we'd fall silent in al-most all conversations! Everyone loves to gossip. It is so ef-fortless and seems so innocent, and the opportunities for it are practically endless. Gossip is especially compelling when we are with friends who we know will agree with our critical as-sessments of others outside our circle—especially when our assessments are humorous and entertaining.

The practice of this precept of not speaking of the faults of others gives us pause and reminds us that gossip isn't as harm-less as it may seem. When we run another person down in his or her absence, we color our feeling about that person, so that the next time we see him or her a pall is cast in our minds. This pall, subtle as it may be, makes it hard for us to face the person with openness and we don't feel clean and honest in the encounter.

The pall extends still further: if you and I gossip about a third party, I can't help but suspect that you may gossip about me with someone else. Maybe you have been doing this al-ready. How can I trust you, knowing that you are capable of speaking this way about someone? (Even though I'm doing it, too!) If that's so, can I trust myself? Do I turn my critical eye and satirical tongue inward as well as outward, diminishing my self-regard? Like a corrosive liquid that slowly seeps through many layers of fabric, gossip's negativity has a way of saturating our hearts and our relationships.

Suppose we took seriously the universal religious teaching that all human beings are potentially loving, kind, and worth-while. Suppose we realized that our not seeing them like that is as much the fault of our own vision as of their imperfection. How then would we speak about them? And suppose we rec-ognized and respected the power of our own speech, knowing that, as Zen master Dogen says, kind speech "can turn the des-tiny of a nation." If we recognized this power, would we ever speak poorly of anyone—even people who richly deserve our reproaches? Wouldn't we rather recognize that everyone—especially those about whom the most terrible things can truly be said!—needs our kind speech and can benefit from it?

In the course of real life as we know it, this seems a tall order. Surely it is not always possible to speak kindly and nicely about everyone. How can you practice kind speech if you are a supervisor needing to give feedback to an employee, or even needing to fire him or her for malfeasance or incompetence? What if you have been forced by circumstances to take on an adversary or defend a position? Aren't these special cases in which this precept might not apply?

I think not. In fact, no matter what you need to say to or about someone in whatever circumstances, it is always possible, and even necessary in the long run, to speak from a heart of kindness and understanding. Even if you need to be critical or speak defensively, there is always a way to do it honestly and in a way that does not express dislike, denigrate the other side, or engage in personal attack. For just as your speech conditions the experience of another person, it also conditions your own experience. If your speech depicts a world populated by bad, incompetent, thoughtless, nasty people, then that's the world you live in, and you will suffer the consequences of it. Truly the world we most intimately inhabit is the world created by our thought and by our speech, which is both the result of and the cause of our thought. As the first verse of the ancient Buddhist text, the Dhammapada, says, "What we are today comes from our thoughts of yesterday, and our present thoughts build our life of tomorrow; our life is the creation of our mind. If a person speaks or acts with an impure mind, suffering will follow as the wheels of a cart follow the beast that pulls it."

Gossip and fault-finding speech can be avoided. There is always a way to speak that communicates what needs to be said without diminishing the mind that sees the potential for good in others. Making the effort to speak like this is one of the best ways to transform our lives.

The Seventh Grave Precept: Not to Praise Self at the Expense of Others but to Be Modest

This is another precept about speech and its power. Not to praise self at the expense of others is to speak about ourselves with modesty, not favoring ourselves too much in what we say. Practicing this precept helps us cultivate a heart that is as concerned about others as it is about itself. Self-centered speech is quite normal—we don't have to be raging egotists for our speech to regularly favor ourselves. In ordinary conversation, how often do we ask about others in anything more than a polite way? And when we do want to hear about others, isn't it often for the purpose of comparing or relating their experience to our own?

When our speaking is habitually focused on ourselves, we are creating a world separate from others. The world in which I occupy the center is a small world indeed. On the other hand, the world in which others' lives are just as important as my own is a world large and various enough for me to grow in. To practice not praising self at the expense of others slowly extends the world in which we live, making it more and more inclusive and less and less in need of defending.

It is easy to see why we so strongly favor ourselves in our speech practice. Because we feel instinctively that our situation is shaky, that we are not as wonderful or as talented as we ought to be—or as someone else is—we are in constant need of praise and confidence-building. Since our experience has been that very few will give us this boost, we feel we need to take matters into our own hands. So much of our posturing and self-promotional speaking has its root in our lack of feeling self-worth. The person who speaks modestly, not favoring self and praising others, is someone who is secure enough not to need extra praise. To practice this precept is to gradually become such a person.

As with all the speech practices, not praising self at the expense of others requires the discipline of paying attention to what comes out of our mouths and honestly observing how our words make ourselves and others feel. The hardest part of the practice is remembering to do it—unconscious speech, we quickly see, is natural and pervasive. But we do get better at this practice. We train ourselves to notice when we are interrupting or monopolizing a conversation; we make the effort to catch ourselves and stop. We train ourselves to ask about how someone else is doing, and then to actually listen to what they say. Can we respond with something truly supportive? Can we be imaginative enough to see the other person's joys, sorrows, and accomplishments as if they were just as real and important to us as our own? And when it is time for us to speak about ourselves, can we do that in a balanced way, without excessive and exaggerated (though probably subtly masked) self-praise?

As we go on with this practice, less self-consciousness and restraint is required. As with all the precepts, the effort eventually becomes quite natural and spontaneous. It begins to seem dull to go on and on about ourselves and never notice others. Self-praise begins to seem foolish. How can we take credit for things—our accomplishments are achieved only thanks to the help of many others. All things depend on each other. Without the food he had for breakfast (produced by the farmer with the aid of rain, soil, and seed and delivered by truck), the highway he drove into town on (paved by workers with the help of machinery manufacturers, administrators, and taxpayers), the clothes he is wearing (made abroad by women working in factories), and many other things requiring cooperation and aid that comes from all over the world, the salesman would not have made the sale that won him the achievement award. This is true of anything anyone has ever done. We can accept credit for our accomplishments, but we must always recognize that we have had countless collaborators.

On the other hand, true modesty doesn't require us to denigrate ourselves. In fact, when we denigrate ourselves and underestimate our skills and talents, we are not keeping this precept but breaking it. The habit of self-denigration is the sneakiest form of self-centeredness. Feeling miserably sorry for ourselves gives us full permission to dwell on ourselves constantly and to seek support from others all the time without having to give back any support in return. Though on the surface they might feel and look different, self-denigration and self-inflation are two sides of the same coin, two ways of putting ourselves at the center of things. These habits of thought and speech may not be easy to break. But when we practice this precept, we begin to recognize them for what they are and see exactly how they create suffering. Then we can begin little by little to break them.

The Eighth Grave Precept: Not to Be Possessive of Anything but to Be Generous

Possessiveness seems like the most natural thing in the world. At a certain age children learn to say "mine" quite emphatically as they yank on a toy that another child is holding. Who doesn't need and want many things? Throughout human history people have been fighting over territory, property, and precious objects. Even the Bible is a tale of getting and fighting to keep. Is it possible—and is it even desirable?—to practice nonpossessiveness? I think it is. As strong as our will toward possessiveness is, just as strong is the knowledge that possessiveness is ultimately tragic, for in the end we cannot keep what we have, and trying to do so makes us anxious, narrow, and mean-spirited.

I have a friend who made a good deal of money a few years ago when the stock market was booming. He became quite obsessive about his holdings and had several television monitors installed in his home so that he could keep close tabs on the fluctuations of the market. When I visited him in his quiet house high up on a hilltop overlooking town, I found it difficult to carry on a normal conversation with him because he was always looking over my shoulder at one of the monitors on the wall and occasionally excusing himself to make an important phone call. As more and more money came pouring in, my friend, who is quite creative, found more and more ways to spend it. When he became interested in thoroughbred horses and bought several, he also eventually needed to purchase a stable for them and hire a crew of people to train and groom them. He took an interest in real estate all over the world and purchased several homes in far-flung countries. He bought yachts, a small fleet of cars, and I am sure many other things I had no idea of.

All of these new possessions seemed to be on his mind constantly. He seemed happy enough, even to be thriving, but he was extremely busy and quite distracted. When the stock market fell sharply and the several businesses he had started crashed to earth, he was busier than ever, but much less happy. I ran into him one day at a restaurant, and he told me that he was continuing to lose millions of dollars every day and that keeping the stables going was becoming increasingly difficult. When I suggested that he save himself the trouble and sell his horses, he looked at me with a deep sadness in his eyes and said, "You don't understand. I love these horses. They mean everything to me. I've put millions of dollars into them. I've got to fight to keep them." Although it was hard for me to understand, he did seem truly desperate about the horses. I felt sorry for him, for it seemed as if his rather spectacular possessiveness had made him miserable.

Few of us will live out our practice of possessiveness quite so dramatically. And yet we can all relate to the misery that comes when we don't get something we want, or when we are in danger of losing something we have. Loss is built into the very idea of possession: possessions are precious exactly because they can be lost. Most of us do not recognize this, and when we experience loss, we become frightened and hold on even more tightly. But if we are wise enough to see that it is painful to deny that loss is inevitably a part of possession, we have a lot of incentive to practice nonpossessiveness. We learn to keep a loose enough hold on what we have that we won't be destroyed when we lose it.

The more we focus on our possessions as the substance and measure of what we are, the more vulnerable we are. When we expand our sense of self to include others—as well as the sky and the wind and the darkness of the night—our possessions do not loom so large in our lives that they actually possess us. We don't have to live in a state of deprivation or renunciation to practice nonpossessiveness. It is possible to practice nonpossessiveness even in the midst of great wealth. The practice of nonpossessiveness has less to do with what we have or don't have than it does with how we understand and live with what we have.

Most of us have a great deal of conditioning about possessiveness. To practice the precept of nonpossessiveness is to work with our conditioning and make the effort to expand our understanding, let go of our habitual concepts and feelings, and loosen the stranglehold they have had on us.

Having lived for so long without much money, I always found it difficult to go shopping and pay the high prices the stores always seemed to charge. I decided that I could work on this by recognizing that when I bought something, I was not, as I had always felt, relinquishing too much of my hard-earned money, scarce as it was. Instead, I was giving money to people who needed it—store clerks, factory workers, farmers. Practicing like this over time, I was able to shift my perspective so that I no longer minded or worried as much about the price I paid for things.

Ultimately, to practice nonpossessiveness is to recognize that it is impossible to possess anything. No one actually owns anything. Things own themselves. They are constantly circulating, passing from hand to hand, transforming, changing shape and location. We work so hard to ensure that our possessions will remain securely in our own hands—installing locks and gates, buying insurance policies, hiring armed guards, making contingency plans. But in the end we die, and all that we have worked for and tried so hard to protect ends up in someone else's hands.

If we don't really possess things, how much less do we possess the people in our lives. The very nature of our relationship to them, if it is a truly loving human relationship, is freedom, even though it may include commitment and obligation. To really love someone—a spouse, a child, a colleague, or a friend—is to recognize that they are not us, that they have needs, aspirations, and lives that do not belong to us and that we cannot control. Can we appreciate and give of ourselves to them without fixating on what they will give us in return? Can we allow them their freedom and autonomy? Love like that may be the highest form of the practice of nonpossessiveness.

The closer we look, the more we see that our lives have

arisen as a result of, and always in connection with, so many others. Our thoughts, feelings, and attitudes come and go, produced in large part by our associations with all that we have encountered in our lives. Even our bodies are a flow that is not really our own, maintained by processes that will transform one day into wind and water, liberated from our thoughts, our wishes, and our histories. At its deepest level, to practice nonpossessiveness is to act on the recognition that our life is always sharing. Knowing this is so, we naturally want to be nonpossessive with material things, with our time and energy and presence, with our words, and, especially, with our love. Nonpossessiveness is the practice of bodhisattvas.

The Ninth Grave Precept: Not to Harbor Anger but to Forgive

This precept is subtle and important. Although all spiritual traditions deal with the question of anger, it seems to be a particular specialty of Buddhism to analyze and discuss anger. Buddhist practice affirms that anger is never a good thing and that we should always let go of it once we are aware of its destructive power.

But this is a tricky business. What about justified anger—anger at social ills, or anger that wakes people up out of their stupor and rouses them to necessary action? I suppose these cases beg the question of exactly what we mean by the word *anger*. If anger is, as I would define it, "the powerful blind impulse to do harm," then it is never justified and it never helps. Although the righteous energy to change unjust social conditions or to rouse someone to take action in his or her life might include some degree of annoyance or ill will, it is not really anger if it comes from a positive motivation. Psychologically, someone whose feelings of hurt or loss have been deeply suppressed may need to rouse a great anger in order to overcome the old emotional blockage. But in this case anger is only a stage, a temporary expedient, whose real root is the original hurt or loss, not the motivation to harm. If the anger goes on for too long or is inappropriately encouraged and so hardens into an attitude of revenge, it would not promote healing—it would only perpetuate and strengthen the initial wound.

Anger more commonly arises when we have been crossed or violated in some way and we do not want to admit this or to experience it fully. In this sense anger is an intoxicant, a cover-up for the painful hurt feelings we can't bear to feel. The practice of this precept doesn't require that we never be angry. That would be impossible—when the conditions for anger arise, anger inevitably appears. In practicing this precept, however, we can make the effort to turn toward our anger when it arises, bearing witness to it and experiencing it fully, but not grabbing hold of it, justifying it, or acting on it. Practicing this precept will give us the confidence and the spaciousness to stop supressing our anger—to see that we can feel our anger and honor it without being consumed by it, that we can allow it and *be* it through and through, giving it space inside to fully manifest, without indulging it.

Anger is usually not pleasant. The eyes bulge out, the heart races, the body is full of tension and pulses with uncomfortable energy. All this can be experienced without causing harm, and it may even be beneficial sometimes. It's not the anger itself that is the problem—it is the grabbing hold of the anger and acting on it that causes harm. There is an old Buddhist saying: "Anger is like a pile of shit: in order to throw it on someone else, you have to pick it up first." And when you do, you are the one who ends up smelly. To practice not harboring anger is to allow ourselves to experience anger, to respect and honor it as a raw and basic emotion without becoming victimized by it.

Unpleasant as it may be, anger can also feel very good sometimes. It can make us feel powerful in the face of the impotence we might otherwise feel when we have been wronged by another. The other person has gotten the better of us and robbed us (it always comes down to this) of our sense of autonomy and worth. This is what hurts—the feeling of being diminished, defeated, weakened. But now that we are angry we are no longer weak—we have become fear-inspiring and powerful. People get out of our way. They may even yield to our demands. This seems much better than being a weakling or a doormat.

But this view of anger as power is based on a mistaken sense of what personal power really is. The power to dominate or overcome is a tragic power in the end, for it is always bound to fail. No matter how strong or clever we are, someone else is always stronger and more clever. No matter how loudly we yell, there is someone else who will yell louder. Holding personal sway over others is always temporary—sooner or later the victor becomes the vanquished. The power to embrace conditions and let go is a much stronger power than the power to dominate. The true source of human power lies in recognizing what we truly are—beings with an infinitely wide scope, who can be limited externally but never internally, except by ourselves. By making imaginative use of whatever happens and cooperating with rather than resisting what is, we do not need to indulge our anger in order to feel strong.

Anger is in the end a marker of our weakness, not of our strength, and this is why it is so useful. Our anger will show us, once we have practiced with it long enough to be able to notice, the limits of our power, for anger always flares up precisely in the places where we are most vulnerable, where the boundaries of our sense of self are most easily challenged. The person who doubts her beauty will get angry when someone suggests that she is not beautiful; the person who feels inadequate sexually will get angry when someone else flaunts his sexuality. Studying our anger shows us those places where we are brittle and defended, where we are weakest and most need to grow. As we practice not harboring our anger, with full attentiveness, we come to see ourselves much more accurately and viscerally. Using our anger well, we can pinpoint our weak points, our personal narrowness, and expand there, so that as our practice progresses and the horizons of our personal power expand, anger arises less often and less virulently.

The positive side of this precept is the practice of forgiveness, which is just this expansion. Working with our anger, studying it, and softening into it, we eventually forgive ourselves for our weaknesses, and that very forgiveness transforms those weaknesses. Although they may not go away, they won't hurt us anymore. Forgiving ourselves also helps us to recognize over time that others who have hurt us are themselves victims of their own narrowness and weakness. As we understand this—and see it directly and immediately in our experience—we more easily forgive others for their hurtful actions. As forgiveness and empathy expand, anger lessens. We don't need to get angry to feel powerful anymore. We feel a truer and deeper power in settling into what is, with compassion and understanding.

The Tenth Grave Precept: Not to Do Anything to Diminish the Triple Treasure but to Support and Nurture It

This precept returns us to the beginning. With the commitment to take refuge in the Triple Treasure of Buddha, dharma, and sangha, we began the journey of the practice of ethical conduct

by recognizing our real and most fundamental human nature—
that we are all, at bottom, awakened, maturing beings who have
it in our hearts to make the effort to become what we most
deeply are. That initial recognition and commitment has led us
to consider step by step how we view ourselves and live in the
world. Along the way we have gradually come to see that our
conduct does count, that all our acts of body, speech, and mind
matter. We have come to see that the more we are aware of our
conduct and work toward clarifying it, turning toward openness
and sharing with others and away from narrow and frightened
self-centeredness, the happier we become, and the happier we
are able to make other people in our lives. We come to see that
the possibilities for refining our conduct and deepening our
view of life are endless.

This final precept affirms and reinforces all that has gone
before. It is all sixteen precepts rolled into one. It reconfirms
us in our pledge to always make an effort to nurture and sustain our highest and deepest commitments and never to
knowingly choose to do anything that would diminish them
in any way.

THE TEN GRAVE PRECEPTS SEEM TO COVER DISCRETE AND
different topics, but in precept practice—as in almost everything else in life—categories and distinctions are only conve-
nient devices that help us reflect on our life and our conduct.
In fact, the precepts are hard to keep separate. They seem to
blend into one another from time to time: nonstealing becomes nonpossessiveness, nonlying becomes not praising self
at the expense of others, and so on. Although in our daily
practice we can focus for a time on one precept or another, in
fact throughout our lives we are constantly practicing all of
them at once. Some say that in reality there is really only one

precept—taking refuge in Buddha, returning to our true capacity and identity as an awakened, caring human being. The precepts offer an infinite variety of ways to practice that fundamental point.

Traditionally it is said that precepts are practiced simultaneously on three different levels: the literal, the compassionate, and the ultimate. On the literal level, we do our best to follow the precepts to the letter. Not killing means not killing—we try our best to kill nothing. The literal level is also quite practical. Knowing we are always living with others in community, we know we need to make an effort to act as peacefully and as harmlessly as possible. We abide by ethical and social codes as straightforwardly as we can—not breaking laws, not offending against custom. We try to reduce our fixation on our desires and satisfactions so that we can promote the greater good.

At the compassionate level of precept practice, we may find it necessary to go beyond rules, laws, or customs, motivated not by willful self-interest but by compassion, which sometimes causes us to transcend the literal level of good conduct for the purpose of helping others. For instance, if telling the truth will hurt someone seriously, we might tell a lie to save that person. If we feel that the world requires us to speak out dramatically against political or social injustice and we need to break a law in the course of doing that, we break the law. Compassion might sometimes require us to act to disturb the peace—to transcend the expected and the approved.

The third level of precept practice is the ultimate level. Through our spiritual endeavors—meditation, prayer, contemplation—we try to penetrate to this level, until we come to appreciate that the precepts are deeper than we have ever imagined: so deep that they can never be completely understood. We come to see that our ordinary, mundane choices and actions are really much more than they seem, reverberating beyond anything we had imagined. On the ultimate level, we appreciate that precepts are beyond breaking and not breaking, distinctions we now see as products of our limited conceptualizing minds. Like the precepts, ultimately we and the world cannot be violated, for we are complete and perfect as we are. At the same time, we and the world are tragically limited—things will always be a little off, and conduct will always fall short. On this ultimate and paradoxical level, it doesn't even make sense to utter the word *precept* or the words *good, bad, self* or *other*. Beyond the dividing narrowness of our limited view, things are connected and complete, and no rules or restraints are required. Appreciating this level (even if only intellectually), we know that we don't need to be hard on ourselves or others for breaking precepts, or congratulate anyone for keeping them. The only important thing is to go on forever making the effort to practice precepts, without measurement or seeking after results. On the other hand, we also see how easy it would be to use the ultimate level as a cover for our self-deception, justifying our willful bad conduct with the thought that "precepts can never be broken anyway, and everything is already perfect." This trap is all too clear. The truth of the ultimate level notwithstanding, we are forever subject to the practical obligations and effects of our actions.

The three levels do not represent a hierarchy of understanding. They are just ways of speaking that help us appreciate the depth and strangeness of life, and to recognize that living ethically is a task that requires our best attention. In the end the long road toward maturity leads us to mystery, the true ground of growing up. Knowing that we don't know doesn't prevent us from trying to know. Knowing that conduct is always ambiguous in an imperfect world doesn't discourage us from trying to conduct ourselves beautifully. The practice of ethical conduct and all the other practices for maturity that we have been discussing bring us to the recognition that truly growing up is more than ordinary, more than natural. It is not a chore, something to be accomplished quickly, so that we can get on with more important things. To walk the road toward maturity is to journey to the center of life's mysterious meaning.

Afterword

B U D D H A ' S
S M I L E

THERE'S A LINE IN THE LOTUS SUTRA I'VE BEEN THINKING about for more than twenty years. It comes at a crucial moment in the narrative, as the Buddha is revealing the esoteric meaning of his teachings to a vast assembly of astonished practitioners. "In the past," the Buddha tells them, "I taught in a linear and straightforward manner about what's wholesome and what's not, about suffering and the end of suffering, about samsara and nirvana. I taught ethical conduct, meditation, and insight, setting forth a path of practice that was clear and manageable.

"But all of this," Buddha confesses, "was merely skillful means I had to use, knowing that it was as much as you were capable of understanding at that time. Now I am revealing a deeper truth—that the path, the teachings, the practice, is much larger than I indicated before—in fact, it is infinite in scope, limitless, because beings are infinite and limitless. Although I defined it before, in truth the path cannot be defined. No ordinary person could possibly know it, for it is beyond all knowing."

Now comes my line: "Only a Buddha and a Buddha," he says, "can understand it." Even a Buddha by himself can't understand it. Only a Buddha *and* a Buddha can. Only through profound relationship, deep encounter, ineffable meeting, can we ever hope to appreciate the immense dimensions of our human life.

Our life is really nothing more than a series of moment-by-moment meetings. When we meditate, we can see this. Slowing down and focusing the mind, we meet what's inside us. Sitting quietly, paying close attention, we meet thoughts, we meet feelings. We meet our breath, we meet sensations in our body. We meet fear, memory, desire, aversion, the oddly taken-for-granted experience of identity. Every moment brings a new opportunity for meeting; every moment is a challenge to remain awake enough, soft and persistent enough, to be present with what comes forth. As our practice continues we see how often we don't meet what's inside us, how much of our life remains hidden to us because we are not willing to let it in. But as we learn more and more that it is possible to be present, even with difficult meetings, our trust in life grows. We are willing to stop trying to control and shape what happens according to our desires. We are willing to meet what comes forth in our life as completely as we can on each occasion.

When we get up from our meditation seat, we meet a more varied world, a world of color, shape, noise, and complexity. Our eyes meet visual objects, our ears meet sounds, our noses meet smell, our tongues meet taste, our skin meets touch. Our minds put together a world out of all this. We meet that world and try to understand and embrace it—to find our place in it. The world calls us forth and we express ourselves. We make choices, and we stand by those choices. We meet mountains, trees, streams, animals, and other people. Coming to maturity in this complicated world is a matter of meeting each thing, inside and out, with sensitivity, awareness, and persistence, with trust, love, and wisdom. We need these qualities in order to fully meet what's in front of us. When we can do that naturally, we find our place in the world.

Zen practice emphasizes the inclusiveness of each moment of meeting. To meet one thing completely, the Zen masters of old tell us, is to meet everything. When Mazu tells us, "This very mind is Buddha," he means that every moment of mind, every moment of meeting, includes the whole of reality. When Dongshan is asked, "What is Buddha?" and he responds, "Three pounds of flax!" he is pointing to the same thing. In Japanese culture, which was profoundly influenced by the Zen feeling for life, it is natural to create art forms out of simple everyday acts like making a cup of tea or arranging flowers, for in these ordinary domestic gestures all that is profound in life can be discovered. The whole world is in one cup of tea; all beauty is in each flower. Each thought in the mind, truly met, contains all that has ever been thought. Every emotion, deeply encountered, contains all that has ever been felt. Every person we meet evokes all of humanity. In the Zen meditation hall we bow to our meditation cushions with this same spirit, honoring the small place on which we are about to sit, knowing it contains all of space and time.

Recognizing the immensity of each moment of meeting doesn't necessarily make life easier. In a way, it makes it more difficult. But there's satisfaction in such difficulty, for it is always real. So often spiritual practice is presented as ethereal and joyful, full of enlightening moments and peak experiences. Such experiences sometimes do occur—we meet them, too, enjoying them without making too much of them. Like all experiences, they pass. The great thing is not a marvelous spiritual experience but an ongoing way of practice that takes into account all of life—its difficulties as well as its joys—and that includes not only our own personal experience but the feeling we can have for others and the world.

If you see life as only positive, only wonderful, only encouraging, you haven't really been paying enough attention. Life is much more than that. There's a famous picture of Shunryu Suzuki Roshi on the back of his book *Zen Mind, Beginner's Mind.* Suzuki Roshi isn't smiling blissfully, as we might expect of a spiritual master. He is simply staring straight ahead into the camera lens, with a determined but amused look on his face that says, "I am meeting whatever comes with interest and patience. Sometimes it will be good, sometimes it will be not so good. But whatever it is, I will be glad to meet it."

One friend who practices Zen with me studied long ago with Suzuki Roshi. He told me: "I came to the Zen Center just a few months before Suzuki Roshi's illness. But in those few months I made such a strong connection because I felt so completely met by him. No one else in my life, before or since, has ever met me that thoroughly. He seemed to be always ready and waiting for me in every encounter—wide open, yet unassuming and quiet. It touched me deeply." I have heard this same comment from many other people who practiced Zen with Suzuki Roshi. So many of them say they still think of him almost every day and feel as if in some strange way he is continuing to meet them even now.

True maturity is being willing and able to show up for all of life's meetings. This takes listening, but also responding—receiving something deeply, trusting life enough to allow that thing to change you, and then coming forward forthrightly, trusting yourself and your instincts. Maturity is knowing that the world is constantly creating you moment by moment, but also that you are creating the world as you come forward to meet it with your skills, talents, and activity.

When we are young, this process of meeting teaches us about the world and about ourselves. So much of what we meet we have never met before, and like the practitioners in the Lotus Sutra assembly, we are astonished by what transpires. Our response to all this input teaches us what kind of people we are—how we think and feel, what's easy for us to do, and what's difficult. We build new worlds; that is how we explore our hearts and minds when we are young.

When we get older, we have seen and experienced more. We've been excited, but we have also been disappointed. We've had many victories and defeats, and we've had the time to reflect on it all, to evaluate and understand. At this point in our lives we learn from teaching others, from passing on to them, as best we can, the fruits of what we have come to know. This is not to say that we have things figured out. Far from it—life teaches us to be humble, to recognize how much we don't know and probably never will know. But from now on we learn as much from being in the presence of others as we do from our own insights and experiences. This sharing and teaching is an important part of the maturing process. Through it we come to some real accord with others. We feel we can entrust them with our spirit, with our sense of what life is about. The culminating moment of the Lotus Sutra comes when the Buddha hands the teachings down, trusting the bodhisattvas to carry it forth after he is gone.

Zen practice puts great emphasis on this sharing and entrustment. More than many other schools of Buddhism, Zen emphasizes the teacher-disciple relationship as the vehicle for understanding, the container that makes maturity possible for both parties. Zen masters are neither teachers in the ordinary sense (possessing knowledge that can be explained or imparted) nor gurus possessing spiritual powers and virtues. Instead, they are, like Suzuki Roshi, seasoned practitioners who are willing to meet other practitioners, each one on his or her own terms. The magic of this meeting—which is neither the teacher's nor the student's doing but exists at the point of contact between them—produces the awakening suggested by the words of the Lotus Sutra: "Only a Buddha and a Buddha can understand." This "warm hand to warm hand" meeting is said to have begun with Buddha and his first disciple and to have continued through the generations down to the present. It is called "face-to-face transmission."

Here is the Zen story of the first transmission from Buddha to Mahakasyapa. Long ago, when the Buddha was at Vulture Peak giving a talk, he held up a flower before the assembly. At this everyone remained silent. Only Mahakasyapa broke into a smile, and Buddha smiled, too. Buddha then said, "I have the treasury of the eye of truth, the ineffable mind of nirvana. I now entrust it to Mahakasyapa."

This is a story of pure meeting. There's no instruction, no test, no program, no content. There are no words, nothing you could put your finger on other than a smile shared between two people who are appreciating together the profound beauty of the flower that is our life.

OUR COMING-OF-AGE GROUP MET REGULARLY FOR ABOUT two years. After two years, just as we were getting to know and appreciate each other, it seemed time to bring it to a close. We discussed rituals that we might end with, because it seemed impossible, after all that we had meant to each other, to simply disband. We had had a months-long discussion of ethical conduct, and the boys were now starting to pay attention to what they were saying, doing, and thinking, in a completely new way. Together we decided that our closing ritual should acknowledge this.

Again, it was Tony who came up with the creative idea. Instead of taking the Zen precepts in the traditional ritual, he would take them as part of a ritual we would create. As we talked this over further, devoting several meetings to the discussion, we saw that we needed more than one ritual in order to reflect the many kinds of relationships that had been developing between us over the two years we had been together. Each boy had established a new relationship with himself, meeting himself for the first time as an adult in an intentional way. Each had also, as a consequence of this, made a new relationship with his parents. (As part of our work, the parents had met with me and with each other from time to time, and each set of parents met with their son to talk over what was going on in the group.) Each boy had also made a relationship with me, and my relationship with each of them was unique. Finally, together, the five of us had made a relationship of deep spiritual friendship that included the limitations of each one as well as the fullness of each one.

In the end we decided that we would have two rituals. One would include all of us as a group—the four boys, the parents, and me. It would be a private ritual to mark the end of our group meetings. After this I would continue to meet with each boy individually to create with him (and with the consultation and participation of his parents) a personal individual ritual that would express his present understanding and commitment for his life. It was in this ritual that Tony would commit himself to the sixteen precepts. As it turned out, the others boys also made similar (though not identical) commitments to an ethical code that they intended to pledge themselves to live by. And so we began the process of thinking through and performing this series of rituals.

All rituals are expressions and transformations. They express a deep feeling we have about our lives, and through that expression they transform us from one state of being into another. If you take religious ordination, you enter the room a postulant, express your intention to devote yourself to your practice, and leave the room an initiate. If you get married, you walk down the aisle as two single people, express your intention to commit yourselves to loving each other, and leave the room transformed into a married couple.

The rituals the boys and I wanted to create were likewise expressions and transformations: they would express our feeling for the work we had done, and they would be rites of passage, the final step through childhood into adulthood. To help us reflect on how to construct the rituals, we studied rites-of-passage ceremonies in different cultures. Such ceremonies usually involve some form of physical ordeal, symbolizing the process of being born into a new life. The ordeal may take days, weeks, or even months to complete. Often there is fasting, sleep deprivation, or other austerities, and there may also be secrecy, danger, or risk. Rites of passage often culminate in the participant receiving a new name to reflect his or her new adult status. Rites of passage, we found, are also renewal rituals, not only for the participants but also for the communities to which they belong. When one more person takes his or her place as a full-fledged adult member of a community, the whole community rejoices, knowing it has a future.

The ritual we settled on took place outdoors, all night long. Beginning at about eleven o'clock on a full-moon night in January, I hiked up the hill overlooking our temple with the four boys. We hiked in silence for about a half hour, gazing around us at the hills and the sea bathed in moonlight. Finally we arrived at our first destination, the particular spot I had picked out for Tony. I told Tony to stay in this spot, to pay attention to his breathing, to quiet his mind, and to watch the dried grass tips waving in the wind, studying them carefully. Then I went on with the other boys. I deposited James in another spot. I also gave him meditation instructions, asking him to pay attention to his body sensation as he looked very closely at the huge boulder in front of him, at all its detail of ridges, cracks, and colors as they dimly appeared in the moonlight. I did the same with the other two boys, giving each one a special spot out of sight of the others and a special meditation practice to stay with all night long. The sky that night was clear, so it was cold and bright. Because of the full moon, fewer stars than usual were visible. The boys were dressed warmly. Each remained in his own place for many hours.

I had asked the fathers weeks before to think about what they wanted to share with their sons on this night. What were the lessons they had learned through their lives, perhaps from their own fathers? What were the stories, the feelings, the failures, the loves or losses, that they would want their sons to hear and to know about as they were preparing to become adults? I hiked once again up the hill in silence with the fathers, bringing each of them to his son. The fathers came with hot chocolate and blankets and sat down with their sons quietly. I left each father-and-son pair alone in their own place. I have no idea what they said to each other, or whether they spoke at all. After a while I returned, and all nine of us hiked silently down the hill in the moonlight.

While all of this was taking place, the mothers had been in one of the large meeting rooms at the temple complex, where there was a good fire going in the woodstove. They talked quietly or meditated, and after a while they began to write letters that I had asked them to compose for their sons, letters that would express their feelings on this occasion. What was it like to give birth to a child, to care for him and to love him, perhaps to center your life and identity around him, and then to give him up, let him enter the wide world alone? As the few stars faded and the dawn came, the nine of us joined the mothers, and we had warm drinks and snacks. We talked on and on for hours about what we had experienced.

After that night I met with each boy individually, starting with Tony, to develop the second ritual, which would be unique for each boy and performed publicly, in the midst of family and friends. Although each of the rituals was slightly different, they all followed a format that seemed right to us. First, the assembled community was led in meditation practice by the boy. We did the practices that had become our own— the bell meditation, the chanting meditation, the incense offering, the quiet breathing. Next I spoke briefly, saying something about my relationship with the boy and something about our group and what it meant to us. Then I turned the floor over to the boy, who spoke of his experience of becoming grown up and of why he had chosen to make the commitments he was about to make, and what they would mean to him in his life.

Then there was precept taking. With Tony I administered the sixteen bodhisattva precepts in the traditional wording. For each of the other boys it was something different, each one coming, through the process of our meeting and deliberating about it, to a particular wording that he felt expressed his understanding and commitment. (For Sam and James, for instance, the idea of "promises" rather than "precepts" or "commitments" seemed right.) After this the parents were called on to speak to this moment in their son's life, and then the floor was opened to all who wanted to speak, beginning with the three other boys, who on each occasion were eloquent in speaking true words about how much they saw and appreciated in their friend. Finally, I gave each boy a new name, following our Zen ritual of ordination names. I calligraphed the name on a scroll in both English and Japanese characters, presenting the scroll and the name at the end of each of the ceremonies.

They were truly wonderful rituals, full of emotion. Each boy on his day felt, I think, something that few of us ever have a chance to feel: completely seen and appreciated, celebrated and revered. The ceremonies were more powerful than I could have hoped. At the receptions that took place afterward, people seemed buoyantly happy, as if all of them had also just committed themselves to a path of adulthood that was firm, clear, and hopeful. In fact our ceremonies impressed people so much that word of our mentoring group spread quickly, and now there are many mentoring groups for both boys and girls being conducted in several Buddhist communities, based on the work we did.

It is now some years since my time with the boys. I no longer see them very much, though I hear about them. After a period of dropping out of high school, Tony went to junior college, where he is studying industrial drawing. Rashid is also in college. I saw James recently at the Green Gulch temple, and we were both very pleased to bump into each other. Mutually amazed, we beamed at one another stupidly for long minutes before either of us could speak. There wasn't much to say, but the feeling was strong. James is also in college now, as is Sam, who is probably the most changed of the four boys. Small and soft when we first started our group, he has turned out to be lanky and quite tall, well over six feet.

Although the time of our closeness is over and probably won't return, I know how precious that time was for the five of us. Our relationships and all that developed from them have had a powerful effect on each of our lives and on the lives of the many other people who appreciated and witnessed what we did together. The other day I saw a bumper sticker that said something like, "Do not doubt that a few committed people, working together, can change the world. Indeed, this is the only way it ever has." Thinking of the four boys and of our time together, I felt the truth of these words.

The journey through adulthood can be lackluster if we only drift, but it can be profoundly valuable if we completely say yes to it and are willing to travel on wholeheartedly—valuable for us, for those around us, and, in some way we cannot really understand, for the whole world. As I came to discover in my time with the boys, and am continually discovering as I go on practicing Zen with others, a necessary part of that journey is communicating the joy of it to others, inspiring them by traveling side by side with them. Like the Buddha stopping and simply twirling a flower, this is the most natural thing in the world. It makes you smile, and it makes others want to smile with you.

Everything we have and enjoy in this lifetime is in our hands only temporarily. It cannot be held for long; it must be passed on. Taking responsibility to see that it is passed on in a good and thoughtful way is the particular joy of the mature person. Every father and mother, every coach or teacher, knows this. When you pass it on, you discover it anew. In the eyes of the other, your own eyes light up.

Selected Mentoring Resources

Stepping Stones Project The Stepping Stones Project is dedicated to bringing Rites of Passage programs into our communities. We recognize the importance and complexity of the transition from childhood toward adulthood and seek to offer guidance and support that facilitates youth forging a new connection to themselves, their community, and the environment. Our programs are for middle school students entering into adolescence and for high school students becoming young adults. We also consult with organizations and schools seeking to create rites of passage within their communities.

> www.steppingstonesproject.org
> (415) 721-9605

San Francisco Zen Center The Coming-of-Age Program inspires, guides, and encourages our children to lifelong spiritual inquiry and engagement, and provides a supportive environment of peer and mentor relationships in which young people ages eleven to thirteen can meet and discuss their views and perceptions of the world around them. This two-year program includes regular meetings, special events, and activities, including a Family Weekend at Tassajara, and culminates in a Coming-of-Age Ceremony. Please contact Barbara Wenger for further details, 415–502–5217 or e-mail **bwenger@itsa.ucsf.edu**

> San Francisco Zen Center
> 300 Page Street, San Francisco, CA 94102
> www.sfzc.org

Spirit Rock Meditation Center Offers a variety of meditation classes & retreats for families and young people.

> Spirit Rock Meditation Center Teen Program
> c/o Family Program Director
> P.O. Box 169
> Woodacre, CA 94973
> 415–488–0164, x227
> www.spiritrock.org

Check your local Buddhist and yoga centers for similar programs around the country.

Acknowledgments

I'd first like to thank the young people in my life who inspired me to consider what it really means to grow up—my sons Aron and Noah, the four boys in the mentoring group, to whom this book is dedicated, the students in the "Racism, What About It?" writing group, and all my students at Tamalpais High School in Mill Valley, California. All of them have shown me what I was incapable of seeing when I was young: the beauty of youth straining to grow. Much thanks also to Barbara Wenger who, with her usual energy and passion, took the work the boys and I did to the next level in establishing Zen Center's Coming-of-Age Program, and to Noah Levine and Ethan Patchell, the first mentors in that program.

Because maturity is such a difficult subject to be clear about, this has been a difficult book to write. I want to thank my old friend and literary agent, Michael Katz, for his vision, persistence, calmness, and sense of adventure. I would especially like to thank my editor, Anne Connolly (also a Zen student), for her brilliant, cheerful, thorough, and tough-minded work, for her firm belief in this project, and for her unerring ability to see the difference between effective and stupid writing. Thanks also to the many other editors and workers at Harper San Francisco, especially managing editor, Terri Leonard, who made the production aspects of the book delightful.